CAMBRIDGE CLASSICAL STUDIES

General Editors

M. I FINLEY, W. K. C. GUTHRIE, D. L. PAGE

VITRUVIUS AND LATER ROMAN BUILDING MANUALS

VITRUVIUS AND LATER ROMAN BUILDING MANUALS

BY

HUGH PLOMMER

Lecturer in Classics in the
University of Cambridge

CAMBRIDGE
AT THE UNIVERSITY PRESS
1973

CAMBRIDGE UNIVERSITY PRESS
Cambridge, New York, Melbourne, Madrid, Cape Town, Singapore, São Paulo, Delhi

Cambridge University Press
The Edinburgh Building, Cambridge CB2 8RU, UK

Published in the United States of America by Cambridge University Press, New York

www.cambridge.org
Information on this title: www.cambridge.org/9780521201414

First published 1973
This digitally printed version 2008

A catalogue record for this publication is available from the British Library

Library of Congress Catalogue Card Number: 72-90487

ISBN 978-0-521-20141-4 hardback
ISBN 978-0-521-10038-0 paperback

CONTENTS

v

ILLUSTRATIONS

PREFACE

Comparison of three Latin technical texts, where so much of the material is common and yet where its arrangement is so varied and unexpectedly altered, is a task for which I am temperamentally ill-equipped. That the result is not even worse than it is I owe chiefly to H. Nohl, whose *Index Vitruvianus* (Leipzig 1876) saved me hours of work, and who in the Mommsen *Festschrift* (1877, see Note 5) convincingly collected the clearest instances of Palladius' indebtedness to Faventinus, besides explaining away most of the apparent arguments that Palladius wrote first.

For the ink illustrations, with which I endeavour to relieve the heaviness of this rather earth-bound paper, I am indebted to Mr B. D. Thompson, Chief Assistant at the Museum of Classical Archaeology.

I am indebted to the Classical Schoolteachers' Conference, held in Cambridge last July, and to the Classical and Archaeological Societies of Manchester University. I tried out parts of this work on all three, and received a fair and tolerant response.

When I refer to pozzuolana, I shall spell it thus, following earlier editions of the *Encyclopædia Britannica*. I have never grown used to 'pozzolana', the modern orthodoxy.

Where I give an exact reference to Vitruvius, I shall normally give it to the pages and lines in Rose's large edition, as in this I shall be following Nohl's *Index*.

When I quote Pliny's *Natural History*, the books of which have been subdivided in various ways in different manuscripts, I cite the smallest paragraphs into which the Teubner text has divided it.

When I began this study – of the content, not the exact text of Faventinus – I hoped that the *lemmata* that I selected would suffice to illustrate my essay upon him. But I at last decided to make things easier for my readers by including a working text of Faventinus (based on Rose) and a translation of my own, neither of which is to be taken as in any sense final. I am trying to keep the issues open, rather than to close them.

H. P.

INTRODUCTION

CETIUS FAVENTINUS, PALLADIUS AND ROMAN BUILDING SCIENCE

The aspiring commentator on Vitruvius is brought up sharp at the very beginning of the manuscripts by his name. The words 'Vitruvii de Architectura' head all the best texts, and he is known simply as 'Vitruvius' to Pliny and Frontinus. By far the best evidence for his cognomen 'Pollio' is found at the beginning of the Compendium *De Diversis Fabricis Architectonicae*,[1] which follows his tenth book in some of his manuscripts, notably the three minuscules, p, v and g, collated by Valentin Rose for his 1867 edition of Vitruvius. Rose prints it, quite rightly, immediately after Vitruvius; for it represents, with some exceptions, an intelligent collection of purely Vitruvian material. It begins, of course, 'De artis architectonicae peritia multa oratione Vitruvius Polio aliique auctores scientissime scripsere'. Its evidence would not be very good, were it as late as most scholars once believed. Marini, for instance,[2] thought it to have been written by Eutropius, at the end of the fourth century (see his discussion at the end of his third volume). Again, scholars were long unable to make up their mind on the relation between our Compendium and a work which shares a great deal of material with it, the *De Re Rustica* of the late author and 'Vir illustris' (as his manuscripts style him – surely a high-ranking noble of the later Empire), Palladius Rutilius Taurus Aemilianus.

We now know, however, that the Compendium is the work of one M. Cetius Faventinus, and that Palladius, whose fifteen books

---

[1] The name seems a bad one. The scope of the work is best given at the end – 'Quantum ergo ad privatum usum spectat, necessaria huic libello ordinavimus.' The compiler limits himself to private architecture, the second of Vitruvius' main divisions. The general MS title seems to be medieval and to be fashioned on the analogy of such works as Theophilus, *De Diversis Artibus*. In fact, the two manuscripts of Faventinus discovered at Schlettstadt and Vienna (see p. 2 below) have titles reading 'M. Ceti Faventini artis architectonicae privatis usibus adbreviatus liber'. This fact, not made very clear by the discoverers, naturally engrossed with the author's name, is properly emphasized by Meinrach Sirch, *Die Quellen des Palladius* (Progr. Freising 1904), p. 29.

[2] Luigi Marini, *Vitruvius* (Rome 1836).

breathe the spirit of the Roman landed aristocracy as it existed under the later Empire, derived all his Vitruvian material not directly from Vitruvius, but from Faventinus, whom modern scholars – Fensterbusch, for instance[1] – tend to put without question as early as the third century. There is no need to repeat here in detail how, soon after Rose's Vitruvius of 1867, the name M. Cetius Faventinus was discovered at the head of the Compendium in two manuscripts, one from Schlettstadt in Alsace (where, incidentally, the work appears as an independent treatise some way before Vitruvius, not merely as an appendix to him), and another in Vienna, and how these discoveries were published by Joseph Haupt.[2] But one must emphasize that H. Nohl in 1877[3] established once and for all the exclusive dependence of Palladius for all his Vitruvian material upon this Compendium of Faventinus.

In a great many cases the statements of Vitruvius, abbreviated and partly rewritten by Faventinus, are still further shortened by Palladius. Typical of such abbreviation are the statements of all three authors on the flooring to be given to winter-quarters (Nohl, p. 68), as follows:

'ad regulam et libellam summo libramento cote despumato redditur species nigri pavimenti' (Vitruvius VII, 4, v); 'ad regulam exaequata planities reddit speciem nigri pavimenti' (Faventinus 26); 'quod exaequatum nigra pavimenta formabit' (Palladius I, 9).

Here, as so often, the sequence is likely to run, as Nohl said, from Vitruvius through Faventinus to Palladius, and Palladius is unlikely to be using Vitruvius directly. Other instances, that I quote later, will make this likelihood a virtual certainty (see e.g. pp. 5 and 20 below). There is never more of Vitruvius in Palladius than in Faventinus, and there is often much less.

But one must be careful not to see the process as one of mere degeneracy. Even Faventinus, on occasion, and still more

---

[1] C. Fensterbusch, *Vitruv Zehn Bücher über Architektur* (Berlin 1964), p. 10. 'M. Cetius Faventinus macht (wohl im 3. Jh. n. Chr.) einen Auszug aus seinem Werk. Durch Benutzung des Faventinus wieder ist er im 4. Jh. n. Chr. dem Palladius bekannt.'

[2] *Abh. Akad. Wien*, LXIX (1871), pp. 3ff.

[3] Palladius und Faventinus in ihrem Verhältniss zu einander und zu Vitruvius, von Hermann Nohl: *Commentationes Philologae in honorem Theodori Mommseni* (Berlin 1877), pp. 64ff.

Palladius could add valuable information to the Vitruvian. They were both intelligent men, who extensively rearranged the material at their command to meet the practical needs of their readers in a different age and with a programme more limited than the Vitruvian. Being intelligent, their scripts demand closer study than the run of late epitomae. But they also promise us more information on the beliefs and practices of their contemporaries. So they are worth study for their own sake, for the light they shed upon later Roman building practice – always with the proviso that they include only what is relevant to private architecture, the second of the two main divisions of the art as given in Vitruvius I, 3, i. Faventinus says of himself at the end, 'Quantum ergo ad privatum usum spectat, necessaria huic libello ordinavimus. civitatum sane et ceterarum rerum institutiones praestanti sapientiae memorandas reliquimus.' But one must acknowledge that for his purposes his Compendium is well organized. It treats, in orderly sequence, of siting, water-supply, building materials, the planning of urban and rustic residences, the construction of their most important rooms, their finish and decoration and finally two useful instruments, the square and the dial. Its Vitruvian spirit is apparent throughout all its rearrangement, nearly always intelligent, of Vitruvian material. At the same time it could easily be consulted by practical builders. Palladius, too, who was, after all, writing a manual for the owner of a large estate, needed a guide only for private architecture; and this explains why he would be content to use Faventinus. He would naturally place most of the building information from him in his introductory book, on the general layout of the estate, returning to him only once or twice in the twelve books of the agricultural year – in May, for instance (VI, 12) for the shaping and drying of mud-bricks, and in November (XII, 15) for the felling of trees and the sorting of timber.

This last section, on timber, well shows how Vitruvian material fared at Palladius' hands and also the sort of information that he added from his own experience. In II, 9 Vitruvius reviews the character of the principal timber-bearing trees. His information, with his 'scientific' explanations omitted, may fruitfully be compared with that in Faventinus and Palladius. He shows first that

the wood of the silver fir has different properties from oak, cypress-wood from elm (Rose 55, 24), and discusses why silver fir is light and yet able to hold up heavy weights in a truss without bending, adding that it can easily rot or burn, that its lower parts are too damp and its upper too knotty, but that its central stretch is very good for joinery (*intestina opera*). Turning to the deciduous trees, he tells us that the oak is tough but easily warped, the winter oak (*aesculus*) useful but spoilt by damp, the Turkey oak (*cerrus*) and beech likely to rot. He continues with the poplar, willow, lime and agnus castus (*vitex*), all white woods, hard and good for carving; with the alder, which never rots and is most useful for foundations in wet places (and thus for every building at Ravenna); with the elm and ash, hard to work, soft and easily warped, but useful in ties and straps; and finally with the hornbeam (*carpinus*), beautifully easy to carve and made by the Greeks into yokes. He now returns to conifers (Rose, 58, 10), first the cypress and pine, which readily warp ('solent esse pandae') but do not decay, and then to the cedar and juniper, with similar properties, except that the cedar contains oil in place of resin. This oil, applied to such things as books, preserves them from pests ('quo reliquae res cum sunt unctae, uti etiam libri, a tineis et carie non laeduntur'). Moreover, cedarwood has a straight grain ('vena directa'), which made it ideal for the image of Diana at Ephesus and also the ceiling-coffers there and elsewhere. Cedars, says Vitruvius, come from Crete, Africa and parts of Syria. The larch, he continues, is known only around the Po and the Adriatic. It rejects pests and also fire. It was found to be non-inflammable by Caesar at Larignum, from which it takes its name. Transported through Ravenna, it is much used in the municipia around Fanum Fortunae (a city, of course, specially well known to Vitruvius!), and would be very useful for eaves-boards in Rome, where it would stop the spread of fire. Finally in Chapter 10, the last of this book on building materials, Vitruvius asks why the 'abies supernas', from north of the Apennines, is so inferior to the 'abies infernas', grown to the south of them. It is because the infernas 'impetus habet perpetuos ad solis cursum', whereas the supernas 'Septentrionali regioni subiecta continetur umbrosis et opacis perpetuitatibus'.

Here, then, are the bones of Vitruvius' account, and Faventinus draws from it practically the whole of his twelfth chapter. He adds only two small, un-Vitruvian details from his own experience – that beechwood is useful in dry places (Vitruvius merely says it quickly rots), and that cedar-oil preserves cupboards or boxes as well as books ('si libri aut clusa eo inungantur'). He also repeats for the cypress and the pine the remark that, following Vitruvius, he has already made about the fir – that they are not easily bent by a load. Here, surely, he shows his independence; for Vitruvius says they are likely to warp. Of course, he omits Vitruvius' 'scientific' explanations and treats Vitruvius' order in his usual cavalier way, beginning with the silver fir (though omitting its use in joinery) but continuing with the larch. It is strange that he should transpose the larch in this way, including the remark about its usefulness for non-inflammable eaves-timbers. Up till now his alterations have seemed deliberate and intelligent; but by moving the larch he gives the end of his chapter a grave ambiguity. Writing of the cedar, he says 'nascitur maxime in Creta et in Africa, et in Syriae regionibus. quaecumque ergo ex parte meridiana caeduntur utiliores erunt, ex parte autem septentrionali proceriores sunt arbores sed cito vitiantur.' The reader would perhaps assume that he was referring to cedars, not epitomizing in a single sentence the whole of Vitruvius' tenth chapter, about the fir forests of the Apennines. Or else, like Palladius, who had no Vitruvius before him, that he was referring to trees in general. And this, after all, seems the best explanation; that Faventinus had indeed decided that Vitruvius' firs merely exemplified a general rule, and that trees grown on southward facing slopes always supplied better timber than those with a northerly aspect.

Already, Faventinus' departures from Vitruvius seem quite interesting. But they are nothing to those of Palladius.[1] He gives, indeed, Faventinus' trees in Faventinus' order; and he often abbreviates Faventinus' remarks. Thus, whereas Faventinus says of the hornbeam 'carpinus in omni opere tractabilis et utilis invenitur', Palladius has merely 'Carpinus utilissima'. Or where, in Faventinus, we are told 'cupressus et pinus ... non cito

---

[1] For Palladius, I have normally used the text of I. M. Gesner (Leipzig 1774). But I have collated the passages I quote with the Teubner of J. C. Schmitt (Leipzig 1898).

pondere curvantur, durant enim integrae semper', in Palladius we find only 'Cupressus egregia'. At the end of his chapter Palladius seems to think Faventinus refers to trees in general in his remark about the difference between northern and southern timbers. For he began the chapter by saying 'Nunc materies ad fabricam caedenda est, cum luna decrescit. sed arbores quae caedentur usque ad medullam securibus recisas aliquandiu stare patieris etc.'; and he now ends it, 'Quaecunque autem ex parte meridiana caeduntur, utiliores sunt; quae vero ex septentrionali, proceriores, sed facile vitiantur.' So far, then, we see him abbreviating Faventinus. But he adds a good deal. Faventinus, as we saw, omitted Vitruvius' remarks that the silver-fir was easily burnt and easily rotted, and that its middle portion was used for joinery. Palladius knows and adds none of this; but he does say that it is called the Gallic tree, that it is a light wood except when soaked, and that it lasts for ever in constructions if kept dry ('abies quam Gallicam vocant, nisi perluatur, levis, rigida, et in operibus siccis perenne durabilis'). In another passage – 1, 13 – Palladius mentions rods of 'lignum Gallicum' as an alternative to cypress for making a firm skeleton for the vaulted ceilings ('camerae canniciae'). According to the Thesaurus, he alone talks of 'abies Gallica'. In 1, 13, he modifies the statement of Faventinus 21 – 'asseres abiegni ad lineam aut regulam aequaliter dirigantur' – to 'asseres ligni Gallici vel cupressi directos et aequales constituemus'. All this seems a most interesting modification of the material.

Yet more interesting are the insertions he makes between Faventinus' notices of the oak and the beech. Unlike Faventinus, he cannot leave out the winter oak (*aesculus*). He calls it a good timber for vine-props and buildings ('aesculus aedificiis et ridicis apta materies'). Apparently, his own experience recommends it for vine-props. Cato had prescribed common oak (17, 1), Varro oak and juniper (1, 8, iv), or had suggested growing cypresses instead, as a continuous *ridica* against the north wind (1, 26). Columella had advised a whole set of trees (IV, 26), none of them the winter oak. Palladius seems to rely then on his own experience here, as he often does elsewhere; most obviously, of course, where he actually contradicts Columella on whom, according to

Pauly–Wissowa, he relies for about a quarter of the material of Books II–XIII. In III, 16, for instance, he tells us that farmers consider Columella's recipe for nursing old vines back to health and strength complete nonsense. He is writing a practical manual, with a mind of his own.

After the *aesculus* he inserts another tree, the Spanish chestnut (*castanea*). This wood, he says, has an admirable solidity and lasts well in the open air and in roofs – perhaps the earliest mention we have of this rôle, so important in our own medieval buildings. He also recommended it for joinery ('operibus caeteris intestinis'). Its one defect is the weight of its timber. Thus Palladius, who did not know, because Faventinus had omitted, Vitruvius' praise of the silver fir for joinery, suggests a completely different tree, the chestnut. Contrast Pliny (*N.H.* 16, 206), who sees nothing to recommend in the chestnut beyond its durability (16, 212), which is less than that of several conifers, and who puts it to no special use.[1]

Finally, among the conifers Palladius inserts information on the pine which he claims to have gathered himself. Faventinus, strictly following Vitruvius, had said of the pine and the cypress that they last for ever ('durant enim integrae semper'). Palladius says that pinewood will not last except in a dry climate, but that he had found that in Sardinia a cure was known for its tendency to rot – viz. that beams of pinewood should be submerged in cold water for a whole year before use, or else buried on the seashore under a pile of sand to be washed by the ebb and flow of the tide ('aut arenis obruerentur in litore ut aggestionem, qua tectae essent, alternis aestibus reciprocans fluctus allueret').[2] One is surprised that the tides are so pronounced in Sardinia. But Palladius' language – 'cui contra celerem putredinem comperi in Sardinia hoc genere provideri' – is not that of a bookworm.

So, from his short account of timber, we draw a picture of Palladius as no mere hack, but rather a practical author in full control of his material, ready to listen to new ideas, with some

---

[1] Unlike the *Thesaurus*, however – *s.v.* Castanea – I do not believe that Pliny applied to the chestnut, oleaster, ilex, hornbeam and poplar the defect of spindly branches for which he condemns the cornel. He seems to me to compare all these trees only for the texture of their timber, and then condemns poplar-wood too, because its texture, already irregular, is reduced to knottiness by pollarding.

[2] 'Ablueret' ('washed away'), V. G. E. Schmitt. But if it washed away the sand, the tide would wash away the timber too.

knowledge of Sardinia and perhaps of Gaul and with a preference for chestnut which foreshadows the Middle Ages.

We find an interesting expansion of ideas between Vitruvius and Palladius, if we turn to the treatment of wine-cellars; and here Palladius at last provides a neat, architectural solution to one of the time-honoured programmes of the Ancients. Vitruvius merely touches the subject, in Book VI, Chapter 9 (Rose, 147).

> Let the press also [he writes], as well as the bathroom, be next to the kitchen, for so it will be easiest to attend to the olives; and let it have the wine-cellar adjoining (*habeatque coniunctam vinariam cellam*), with windows on the north side. For if they are on any other, then the sun's warmth will have a chance to penetrate, and the wine in the cellar, upset by the heat, will lose its strength. But let the olive-store have windows on the south.

He then describes the space needed for one or two presses, before going on to sheep-pens. Faventinus 13 says that the *cella vinaria* must face the coldest regions of the sky and be lit by northward-facing windows, so that on all sides cold air may preserve the wines. For everything is ruined by hot air (*vapor*). So Faventinus, while keeping Vitruvius' prescription for the cellar, omits his instruction to place it beside the kitchen.

Palladius (I, 18) would have it a long way from almost everything. But all his information is his own. He does not even prescribe the mechanical press (*torcular*) envisaged by Vitruvius and Faventinus, but a treading-floor (*calcatorium*). This seemingly retrogressive feature will tell us little. As is well known, large numbers of slaves can be found at any date in any part of the Roman Empire, and upheld its basic economy. Machines, even *torcularia*, would be by contrast expensive toys. His instructions run as follows:

> We must have our wine cellar facing north, so as to be cool and dark – or as dark as possible – a long way from the baths, the stalls for animals, the furnace, or the middens; from cisterns, from pools, or anything else that smells bad. So well-appointed that it can take any vintage.[1] Now it must be arranged to look

---

[1] The Latin here is obscure to me – 'ita instructam necessariis, ut non vincatur a fructu'. Fortunately, the general sense of the passage is not affected.

like a veritable basilica, with the floor where the grapes are trodden built at a higher level. There should be three or four steps up to this floor between two lakes, sunk on either side of them to receive the must.[1]

Masonry channels or earthenware pipes are to run from these 'lakes' around the outer edge of the walls, and to supply the large earthenware pots placed outside and below them with the running juice, as it trickles down the adjacent stretch of channel.[2] If there is a big supply of wine, then the open space in the middle will be given over to barrels. So that these do not hinder our walking around, we can place them on fairly high platforms or above sunken pots fairly far apart, so that, if necessary, the man in charge can pass between them.[3] But if we do assign a place to the barrels, let it be built like the treading floor with low kerbs and a tiled pavement, so that even if a barrel is leaky and spills out (unknown to the caretaker), the wine that has escaped will flow into the 'lake' below, and not get wasted.[4]

The illustration, Fig. 1, is an attempt to realize this basilical wine-cellar of Palladius. It was not very easy to show the slight downward slope of the two platforms in the 'nave' towards the two 'lakes' at the inner end. You are asked to remember its existence. The cellar is evidently intended for ordinary wine, the sort stored in barrels and not in amphorae. There is thus no worry about storing special vintages. The earthenware pots were needed during the fermentation. I expect they were sunk, partly at least,

---

[1] 'Sic autem dispositam ut basilicae ipsius forma calcatorium loco habeat altiore constructum, ad quod inter duos lacus, qui ad excipienda vina hinc inde depressi sint gradibus tribus fere aut quatuor ascendatur.'

[2] It seems best to give the Latin in digestible stretches. Palladius continues: 'Ex his lacubus canales structi vel tubi fictiles circa extremos parietes currant, et subiectis lateri suo doliis per vicinos meatus manantia vina defundant.' 'Extremos parietes' could mean 'the edges of the walls' or 'the end walls'. In any case the 'lakes' have got to be in the floor of the main building, and the juice has to trickle from them to jars at a lower level. I am tempted to alter 'extremos muros' to 'externos muros' – the outsides of the walls.

[3] 'Si copia major est, medium spatium cupis deputabitur, quas, ne ambulacra prohibeant, basellis altioribus impositas, vel supra (obruta) dolia possumus collocare spatio inter se longiore distantes, ut (si res exigat) curantis transitus possit admitti.' Schmitt, following T, reads 'asellis'. But what have small donkeys to do with it?

[4] 'Quod si cupis locum suum deputabimus, is locus ad calcatorii similitudinem podiis brevibus et testaceo pavimento solidetur, ut etiam si ignorata se cupa diffuderit, lacu excipiantur (non) peritura vina quae fluxerint.'

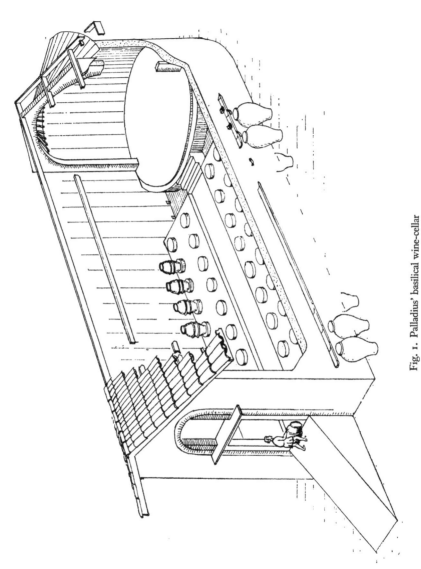

Fig. 1. Palladius' basilical wine-cellar

N.B. The ridge pole and other timbers in this building were inadvertently given modern scantlings. Ancient ridge poles and rafters had approximately square cross-sections.

in the ground. The fermented wine would go into the barrels. The whole process resembles that in the Villa of Boscoreale, near Pompeii.[1] But Palladius' building seems much simpler and more elegant. At the same time, Boscoreale explains several things not clear from Palladius, who could, of course, be abbreviating an earlier writer.[2] Above all, it shows that the large pots, or *dolia*, to hold the must in the later stages of fermentation, would be out-side. The juice would trickle from the 'lakes' (2 and 3 in Room P on Mau's plan) to a channel outside, from which it would be tapped into the *dolia*. For the shapes of the *dolia* and the barrels, our figure relies on the late Roman examples in Daremberg–Saglio, *s.v. dolium* and *cupa*.

Palladius, unlike Vitruvius, gives no dimensions for his little building. But in its main lines, as we have tried to reconstruct it, it seems to fit fairly well into the general pattern of later Roman architecture. The elements of the programme are all to be found not only at Boscoreale but already in Varro, *De Agricultura* I, 13, vi, which says that the pavement of the *cella vinaria* should slope into a 'lake', because the must in its first fermentation is likely to burst barrels (*arcae*) in Spain or earthenware pots (*dolia*) in Italy. But I know of no elegant provision for the whole process before this little basilica of Palladius.

The heating-plant of Baths seems to grow simpler between Vitruvius and Palladius. At the same time, the later writers add each some details and fittings not mentioned by Vitruvius; and they show again that they have a private establishment in mind rather than the services of Vitruvius' public baths.

Vitruvius (v, 10, i) prescribes that men's and women's hot baths should be adjacent, so as to use the same heating vessels and furnace.[3] Three bronze vessels, he continues, should be placed

[1] Mau–Kelsey, *Pompeii* (Macmillan 1899), pp. 355ff. The recent excavation of numerous villas south and east of Pompeii, well summarized by K. D. White (*Roman Farming*, pp. 434ff. and an appendix, pp. 442–5), has produced no solution of this planning problem markedly different from that at Boscoreale (now called 'Boscoreale 13').

[2] For example, the enigmatic but important Q. Gargilius Martialis, whose influence upon Palladius is examined in the article on Palladius in Pauly–Wissowa. It would be consistent, perhaps, with Gargilius' medical approach to these matters to insist on the hygienic isolation of the basilical wine-cellar.

[3] Such should be the meaning of the clause, hard to translate and, I think, corrupt, 'sic enim efficietur ut in vasaria et hypocausis communis sit earum utrisque.' (How does one translate, or even construe 'in vasaria'? Read, perhaps, 'infusoria...communia sint'.)

above the furnace, one for hot water, one for tepid and one for cold. (Modern scholars seem agreed that this should be his meaning, though I must admit that he uses the same words – *caldarium*, etc. – for the vessels as he does for the actual baths filled from them.)[1] They are to be so arranged that the exact amount of water leaving the tepid for the hot may flow into the tepid from the cold, and so that the 'tortoises' of the hot bathing-pools may be heated from the common furnace.[2] These testudines were discussed convincingly by Mau in the context of the Stabian Baths at Pompeii (Mau–Kelsey, *Pompeii*, pp. 185ff), where the bathing-pool in the men's hot bath could contain ten bathers, and where a sunken half-cylinder, opening off one side of the pool, rested immediately above a special flue from the adjacent furnace. The arrangement in this building is very Vitruvian in its juxtaposition of the men's and women's baths and the way in which they share a single furnace. So I have little doubt that Mau's interpretation of the testudo as the sunken half-cylinder is correct, and much prefer it, for instance, to Granger's idea (*ad loc. Vitruvii*) that it was the vaulted chamber containing the bath-basin – on the analogy of the testudinate *atrium* of VI, 3, i, also boldly translated by Granger as 'vaulted', whereas the normal Vitruvian for a vault is *cameratio* or *concameratio*.

The diagram, Fig. 2a, attempts to show the Vitruvian heating-system for the bath-water, with the large vessels in a line, separating the men's and women's baths.

Vitruvius refers later to domestic baths in country houses, but says nothing about them, except that they should adjoin the kitchen (VI, 6, ii). Countrymen will find this the most convenient place for a wash.[3] The kitchen, of course, was virtually the servants' living-room; and Columella (*R.R.* I, 6, iii) says that *familiares* should spend most of their time there. But on the complexity or simplicity of these baths Vitruvius says nothing.

Faventinus (16, *ad fin.*) takes up this advice of Vitruvius, though subtly altering the reason – 'in villa rustica balneum

---

[1] 'aenea supra hypocausin tria sunt componenda, unum caldarium, alterum tepidarium, tertium frigidarium.'

[2] 'testudinesque alveolorum ex communi hypocausi calfaciantur.'

[3] 'balnearia item coniuncta sint culinae, ita enim lavationi rusticae ministratio non erit longe.'

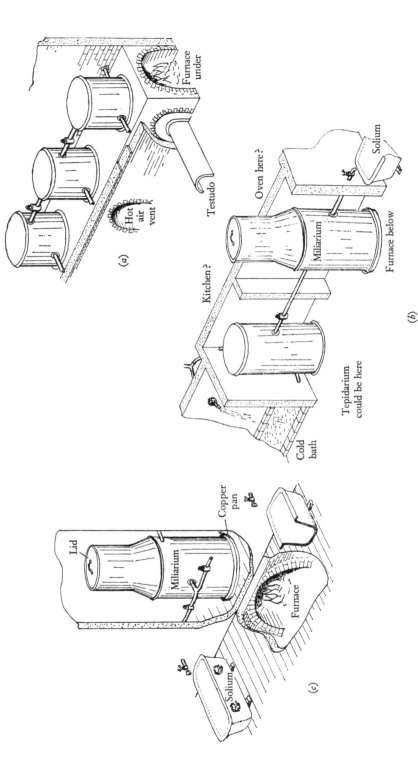

Fig. 2. Heating system for baths, according to our three authors: (a) Vitruvius, (b) Faventinus, (c) Palladius

culinae coniungatur, ut facilius a rusticis ministerium exhiberi possit' – so that if the owner cares to take a bath, he will always be sure of having rustics at hand to wait on him. He also repeats Vitruvius' generalities about lighting and aspect. But his heating arrangements differ. For his bath dispenses with a *tepidarium*, and also substitutes a long bath-tub (*solium*) for Vitruvius' bathing-pool. He also specifies the kind of heating-vessels that he wants. 'Let a leaden vessel, standing on a shallow bronze pan,[1] be placed above the furnace, and another similar one beside the cold bath, so that as much water may be poured cold into the hot vessel as it loses already heated to the bathtub.'[2] If I have translated him correctly, Faventinus' heating system should resemble the diagram, Fig. 2*b*. The bronze stew-pan will offer a minimal pro-tection to the lead vessel, with its low melting-point. This is all, it seems, an intelligent alteration of Vitruvius to keep in touch with Faventinus' own times and needs.

Palladius' system (*De R.R.* 1, 40) seems even simpler, and yet it is explained more technically.[3]

Then indeed we are to place a large cylindrical lead vessel, with a bronze dish beneath it, outside the bathroom wall and between the places where the bath-tubs are to go. It is to stand above the furnace. We are to bring to this vessel a pipe con-taining cold water, while from the vessel a pipe of similar size is to run to the bath-tub, bringing to it at a good heat as much water as the other pipe has brought cold into the vessel.

Palladius is the first of the three writers to call the vessel by its technical name of '*miliarium*'.[4] I am not sure how many bath-tubs

[1] The Latin could be ambiguous; and one could suppose that the vessel had a bronze lid. But common likelihood and the analogy of Palladius (see below, this page) favour my translation. (I have to admit that Faventinus often found it as hard to write Latin as did Vitruvius.)

[2] 'plumbeum vas quod patenam aeream habet supra fornacem conlocetur, alterum simile frigidarium secus ut quantum caldae ex eo in solio admittatur tantum frigidae infundatur.'

[3] 'miliarium vero plumbeum, ciu aerea patina subest, inter soliorum spatia forinsecus statuamus fornace subiecta, ad quod miliarium fistula frigidaria dirigatur, et ad hoc ad solum similis magnitudinis fistula procedat quae tantum calidae ducat interius, quantum fistula frigidi liquoris intulerit.'

[4] Already used, however, by Columella and Seneca. See the *Thesaurus, s.v.*

it is to supply. One, or two? In his arrangement of tubs, Palladius seems to differ from Faventinus; and the diagram, Fig. 2c, tries to reveal the differences.

Each writer, then, pictures the arrangements in his own way.

Finally, Palladius adds two important prescriptions; the first that, if possible, the waste bathwater should be used to irrigate cultivated land (1, 41, iv); the second that one should place one's winter apartments above the bathrooms (1, 41, v). 'Possumus etiam', he observes, 'si compendio studemus' (if we study economy), 'hiberna aedificia balneis imponere: hinc et habitationi teporem submittimus, et fundamenta lucramur.' As over his wine-cellar, he displays a true architectural instinct. His prescription will hardly serve to date him; for massive vaults under large Roman houses, perhaps even including bathing suites, are at least as early as Nero's Golden House. But at least it shows his aware-ness of decent building outside the Vitruvian tradition, and of the type of plan that culminates, for us, at Spalato.

If we turn to the substructures and floors of bath-buildings, we find that Faventinus makes a considerable break with Vitruvius, and that Palladius is as independent of Faventinus. Vitruvius (v, 10, ii: Rose 125) prescribes as follows for the hanging-floors of hot bathrooms. Line the ground with tiles $1\frac{1}{2}$ foot square, giving it sufficient slope to allow a ball to roll down to the furnace-mouth.[1] This will encourage the flame with an updraught. Arrange above this your pillars of eight-inch bricks, so disposed that tiles 2 foot square can span them above. The pillars them-selves should be 2 foot high, and the two-foot tiles above them will support the pavement.

Faventinus (16) follows Vitruvius closely for the lower floor and its slope. But he adds that the pillars, still of eight-inch bricks, should be rounded ('supraque laterculis bessalibus et rotundis pilae instruantur' Rose, emending the 'vel rotundis' of MSS; whereas Krohn, in his usual dreary fashion, excises 'vel rotundis'[2]), and that in a private bath they should be $2\frac{1}{2}$ foot high, in a public bath 3 foot. They are still, however, to be spanned by tiles 2 foot

[1] In this discussion I follow the Roman practice and use the words 'brick' and 'tile' interchangeably.

[2] F. Krohn, *Vitruvius de Architectura* (Teubner 1912).

square. Clearly, building experience had recommended to Faventinus an hypocaust loftier and less encumbered than the Vitruvian.

Palladius (1, 40, ii) lines the ground with two-foot tiles, as opposed to the eighteen-inch tiles of the others. He keeps the slope for the ball. Above, his pillars are to be 2½ foot high, like those of Faventinus, but only 6 inches across. For they are spaced 18 inches apart, and support the usual two-foot tiles. Above these, Palladius' floor is more sumptuous. There are to be two layers of the two-foot tiles, and paving stones above these, and then, if one gets the chance, slabs of marble – 'supra has pilas bipedae constituantur binae in altum, atque his superfundenda pavimenta, et tunc, si copia est, marmora collocentur.'

By the end of the series, only the slope of the floor, the ball and the furnace-mouth survive from Vitruvius; and with Palladius the floor has become as heavy as it reasonably can on supports as slight as safety will require. It would be interesting to see if archaeology confirms this general development.

The most interesting and original piece of building lore in Palladius, apparently unparalleled in any ancient writing, is his chapter (1, 8) on the foundations of his country house, or *praetorium*, as he calls it. This sense of 'praetorium' is found often in Suetonius, and seems redolent of the later Empire. But its foundations, as Palladius describes them (Fig. 3), recall Classical Greece. His ideal country house, if it comes to any harm, should be reparable, he says, with the income of one or two years. Its site should be high and dry. The foundations will be safer so, and the prospect better. The foundations themselves should spread half a foot beyond the walls on all sides. Where cut in the rock, they should be 1 or 2 foot high. When in good clay, the hidden foundation should have a proportion to the height of the building above ground of one to five or six. In looser earth, carry the foundations down to clay. But, if this is lacking, bury altogether one fourth of the building.[1] This all seems peculiar to Palladius;

---

[1] Fundamenta autem hoc modo ponenda sunt, ut latiora sint ex utraque parte semipedis spatio, quam parietis corpus increscet. Si lapis vel tofus occurrat, facilis causa est collocandi, in quo sculpi tantum fundamenti forma debebit, unius pedis altitudine vel duorum. Si solida* vel constricta invenietur argilla, quinta vel sexta pars altitudinis eius, quae supra terram futura est, fundamentis deputetur. Quod si terra laxior fuerit, modo maioris

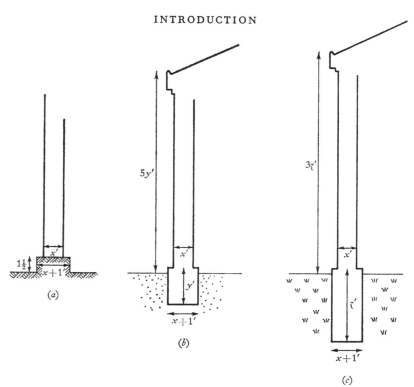

Fig. 3. Rules for foundations, according to Palladius: (a) on rock, (b) on clay,
(c) on loose ground

and I hope it fully justifies my argument for his value as an authority on Ancient architecture. Excessively studied during the Renaissance, he has now been unjustly neglected, because of his late date. But even this helps to give him great interest; for an intelligent, practical writer of the later Empire is always something of a godsend.

I have still to venture on dates for Faventinus and Palladius. Before finally hazarding an opinion, we may well explore what they both have to say on concrete building and on the water-supply. For it is here that building skill achieved some of its most spectacular triumphs, at the hands of the great Imperial builders, in the three-and-a-half centuries after Vitruvius.

altitudinis obruantur, donec munda sine ruderum suspicione occurrat argilla; quae si omnino desit, quartam mersisse sufficiet.'
    * 'solida et constricta' Schmitt.

Concrete, unhappily, is a difficult topic. For one thing, its
ingredients in Central Italy were different from those elsewhere,
and permitted vastly greater virtuosity; and we are not, of course,
at all certain for what area of the Empire either author is writing.
For another, the true court style of building in Roman concrete
came to an end with the reign of Constantine. The Basilica of
Maxentius was its swansong, and Sta Costanza its last degenerate
echo. If Faventinus wrote, as he may well have written, in the
later fourth century, true Imperial architecture was for him a thing
of the past. Finally, there is the ambiguity of the word *structura*,
used indiscriminately by our writers. It can mean either ashlar
masonry or concrete, and the context does not always make the
meaning clear to us. Vitruvius seldom recommends a concrete
structure – he lived too early. He does, however, for rainwater
cisterns, in VIII, 7, xiv (Rose 211). If water lies too deep in the
earth, then supplies of it are to be directed into concrete works
('signinis operibus excipiendae') from roofs and lofty places
('ex tectis aut superioribus locis'). The sand for these works
should be the purest and roughest possible, and the individual
pieces of *silex*, which form the aggregate in the concrete, should
never weigh more than one pound. Miss Blake discusses these
prescriptions in her first volume,[1] and concludes that Vitruvius'
opus signinum contains a true hydraulic cement. The actual cement
is to be made, continues Vitruvius, from two parts of lime to five
of sand, and to be mixed in a trough. The cistern is dug out, and
its walls and floors are beaten hard, before being lined with the
opus signinum. It is desirable to divide the cistern into compart-
ments, to allow for a settling-tank. If there is no space for this, a
little salt should be added.

This advice is all transferred by Faventinus (Chapter 4) from
cisterns to wells. He omits cisterns altogether. Evidently he lived
neither in a dry climate nor a typical limestone region! Vitruvius
dealt with wells immediately before cisterns and merely prescribed for the lining of walls when dug, that it should be of
structura and that care be taken not to wall up the actual spring
with it! But Faventinus recommends *opus signinum* for wells, and
is most detailed. The aggregate should be of silex or tufa (the

[1] *Ancient Roman Building Construction in Italy*, I, pp. 347–8.

18

latter not mentioned by Vitruvius).[1] Two parts of lime should be
mixed to five of rough sand in the trough. The well-shaft as dug
should be 8 foot in diameter, its walls 2 foot thick, and the clear
space therefore 4 foot across. When you begin the 'structura',
you should ram it home with wooden poles, taking care not to
spoil the appearance of its exposed face. Made more solid by such
means, the 'structura' will be more damp-proof.[2] Faventinus then
applies to his well the Vitruvian prescription for cisterns – if the
water is rather muddy, add salt to it. Surprisingly, he now adds
his own correction of 'the authors'' (viz. Vitruvius') prescription.
Although 'the authors' recommended two parts of lime to five
of sand, people have now found it better to mix one of lime to
two of sand. The cost will be greater, but the aggregate will be
more firmly bound together.[3] Finally, you are to proceed in
exactly the same way with brick-faced concrete 'similiter et in
testaceis operibus facies'. Faventinus adds as an afterthought that
while digging a well in crumbling soil, when hampered by red
sand, unstable black earth or sweating damp, you are to hold back
its walls with planks, retained in position by horizontal cross-bars.[4]

So Faventinus appeals to the practice of his own time to correct
Vitruvius, and his prescription profits considerably from the
development of Roman concrete. Concrete construction was still
a living art when he wrote, and extends to *opus testaceum*. While,
of course, Vitruvius knew that walls had been made of baked
bricks or earthenware, notably in Babylon ('latere testaceo

---

[1] Clearly, whatever the original meaning of *opus signinum*, there was no need by this
time to include pounded earthenware in the aggregate. That was reserved for *structura
testacea*.

[2] 'vectibus ligneis densabis sic ut nitorem frontis non laedas. sic enim solidata structura
adversus umorem fortior erit.'

[3] 'sed licet auctores ad quinque partes harenae duas partes calcis mitti docuerint, †isdem
mensuris et redivivas expensas fieri monstraverint†, melius tamen inventum est ut ad duas
harenae una calcis misceatur, quo pinguior impensa fortius caementa ligaret.'
Some of this is surely corrupt. I should myself write 'monstraverunt', and follow it
with a full stop. We could then understand that 'Although authors (*sc.* Vitruvius) have
recommended a mixture of five to two, authors (not Vitruvius) have shown that with this
mixture you'll have a lot more to spend later on. So a better mixture was found, of two
to one, so that a greater (initial) expenditure might bind the aggregate more firmly.' Krohn
excises the whole passage, but without MS warrant. He would deny all originality to
Faventinus – a perverse hope. After all, at the outset, Faventinus does claim to know
authors besides Vitruvius.

[4] 'si terra solida non fuerit aut harena rubrica aut sabulo fluidus aut exsudans umor
fossionem resolvet, tabulas axium directas fodiendo submittes et eas vectibus ligneis
transversis distinebis.'

structum murum Semiramis circumdedit Babyloni' – Rose 196), he confines his own use of it to the cornices of mud-brick walls (Rose 53) or to pavements. Faventinus thus reveals the progress of building under the Empire, during which, especially in the second and third centuries, *opus testaceum* became almost universal in Central Italy.[1]

Palladius in Book IX, Chapter 9 simply abbreviates Faventinus on well-making, and adds nothing. It is perhaps significant that he drops all mention of concrete or brickwork. On the other hand, he discusses cisterns in his initial book (I, 16–17), and says a great deal about them, quite independent of Vitruvius. We must, he says, site our villas high, and escape the lure of well-watered but unhealthy valleys. So, if a spring or well is not at hand, we must construct cisterns. A good cistern (I, 17) will be oblong and have concrete walls ('signinis parietibus'). Its floor will have a deep foundation of packed rubble. A place will be left for drains, and the floor then smoothed with a pavement of tiles, to be carefully polished and wiped down with burnt fat. Such seem to be Palladius' instructions, though he uses the strange expression, 'testacei pavimenti superfusione levigetur'. 'Superfusio', a rare, late word, suggests not ordinary tiled floors but viscosity. The material should correspond to the concrete with earthenware aggregate found even in Augustan times, as shown by Miss Blake (*Ancient Building Construction in Italy*, I, p. 295) and supposed by her, perhaps wrongly, to be the 'structura testacea' used, according to Vitruvius II, 7, xvii (Rose 52), on the tenement blocks of his own day. Palladius next recommends a thorough drying-out of the cistern and a similar polishing of its walls. Then, instead of Vitruvius' settling tanks, he recommends the introduction of eels and fish to give the semblance of running water! There follow complicated recipes for caulking the cracks, which might occur anywhere ('Si aliquando, in quocumque loco, pavimenti vel parietis tectura succumbat'). For he does not really trust the strength or cohesion of his concrete and relies on waterproof linings (*malthae*). He advises the use of earthenware pipes and covered cisterns. Rainwater, he concludes, is best; and river water

---

[1] At the same time, there are difficulties in knowing what exactly is meant by *opus testaceum* and *structura testacea*. See below.

should be used only for washing and irrigation – a prescription which may remind the modern traveller of the motive behind certain early Byzantine cisterns.[1] Thus Palladius, elaborate as are his instructions, especially for lining and waterproofing, and familiar as he is with such ointments as *axungia*, unknown to Vitruvius, does not rely upon the quality of his concrete; and he nowhere considers its composition as Faventinus does. He seems not really to know concrete-mixing, as practised by the best builders before *ca.* AD 320.

For the most obvious remaining clue on the topic of concrete we return to our various authors' bath-buildings, and study their vaults. Vitruvius in Book V, Chapter 10 (Rose 125–6) advocates a kind of shell vault; and while he uses some concrete, his use is tentative. Some sort of stone-built vaults, he says, will be more useful. But, if instead, wooden trusses are used, they must have earthenware work below them, as follows.[2]

> Make straight rods or hoops (*arcus*) of iron, and suspend them from the wooden truss by iron hooks in as many places as possible. And let them be so spaced that tiles made without raised edges can rest upon any two of them. Complete the vault in this way, and then smear its upper surface (extrados) with clay strengthened by hair, and its under side, which faces the pavement, first with a mixture of earthenware and cement ('testa cum calce') laid on with the trowel and then with white-wash or plaster to give a polished surface. Such vaults in hot baths, if doubled, will stop the steam from rotting timber in the truss. For it will be caught and wander between the two vaults.[3]

I do not know any actual instance of such double vaults; but Vitruvius' description seems clear enough.

He returns to the subject of vaults and prescribes for them in general in Book VII, Chapter 3 (Rose 166), this time recommending a wooden frame. In this case, straight wooden poles ('asseres')

---

[1] Notably that of Seleucia ad Calycadnum (Silifke), a magnificent structure only a few hundred yards above the river, but apparently destined for rainwater only (*Monumenta Asiae Minoris Antiqua*, III, pp. 4–6).

[2] 'concamerationes vero si ex structura factae fuerint, erunt utiliores, sin autem contignationes fuerint, figlinum opus subiciatur, sed hoc ita erit faciendum.'

[3] 'eaeque camerae in caldariis si duplices factae fuerint, meliorem habebunt usum. Non enim a vapore umor corrumpere poterit materiem contignationis, sed inter duas cameras vagabitur.'

– of cypress-wood, for silver-fir quickly rots – are to be placed 2 foot apart, giving the shape of a tunnel ('ad formam circinationis'). Attach them to the truss above with ties of wood not easily rotted, such as box, juniper, olive, hard oak (not ordinary oak), or cypress: and fasten everything with an abundance of iron nails. Then tie pounded reeds (preferably Greek) to the rods, as the contour of the vault requires. Then on the extrados of the vault place a layer of mortar, of mixed sand and lime, to throw off any water dripping from the truss above. (Some alternatives follow for work where Greek reeds are not available.) Then apply rough cast to the underside of the vault with a trowel, then spread the sand-mortar and finally apply a polished coat of marble plaster.

All this reinforcement of vaults in Vitruvius seems very neat and natural. The wood or metal skeleton, or ribs, and the web of concrete, tiles, or reeds are both of equal importance. Indeed, no Roman ever outgrew the need to reinforce his concrete vaults with at least some built-in ribs, however good the concrete became, however princely the designs. Again, it would be interesting to find if any vaults are known at all close to Vitruvius' prescriptions. But we have the narrower task of finding whether Faventinus or Palladius felt the need or inclination to depart from them.

Faventinus, in Chapter 17, varies the beginning of Vitruvius on the vaults of bathrooms. 'camerae structiles fortiores erunt. figulinae autem ad contignationem suspendantur.' It seems hard to believe that Faventinus is not here distinguishing between vaults of masonry, or at least with stone aggregate, and vaults largely of earthenware composition. He continues: 'But let earthenware vaults be suspended from the truss in such a way that their earthenware tiles, attached to firmly anchored ties, may hold up like a small mantle the vaults that they round off. You will follow the same method in making flat vaults.' What does he mean by 'flat vaults'?[1] I pictured at first those conical vaults with flat sides which were so popular in the *frigidaria* of baths, from the Stabian Baths at Pompeii onwards (Mau–Kelsey, *Pompeii*, p. 185, Fig. 82), and of which the latest and perhaps the most

---

[1] 'figulinae autem ad contignationem suspendantur ita ut catenis ancoratis fixae tegulae velut palliola quae cameram circinent sustineant. eadem ratione et planas cameras facies.,

famous example is the Baptistery of Pisa Cathedral. But in Chapter 25 it seems to mean only smooth vaults without stucco reliefs.

After this interesting beginning, Faventinus follows the Vitruvian prescriptions very closely until nearly the end of the chapter, when he decides to alter and reinterpret Vitruvius' double shell vault. 'The work will seem', he says, 'both more careful and more useful, if the vaults of bathrooms' (not just hot baths, notice) 'are made double, the lower of concrete, the upper a suspended vault.'[1] He then says that the damp (not the steam) imprisoned between the two vaults will not harm the roof trusses. Also that 'sudationes etiam praestabuntur meliores'. By 'sudationes' he should mean 'sweating-rooms', as does Vitruvius in v, 10, v ('laconicum sudationesque sunt coniungendae tepidario'). But his prescription is too brief for me to understand.

He returns to vaults in Chapter 21, and prescribes for *camerae canniciae*. One must begin with an arrangement of firwood poles. These should be not more than three fingers thick and spaced at equal intervals. Faventinus thus ignores Vitruvius' preference for the cypress and his objection to the fir. He specifies, as Vitruvius does not, the scantling of his deal poles; and he alters Vitruvius' spacing of 2 foot to 1½ foot.[2] The prescriptions for the bundles of reeds seem to differ from those in Vitruvius; but the passage is too difficult and technical for me to discuss. Faventinus does seem, however, to ignore the extrados of the vault, and to concentrate on the coats for the visible underside. Here, more precise than Vitruvius, he recommends a first coat of pumice applied by hand, then a sand and lime mortar and finally a coat of ground marble.[3]

[1] 'maior tamen et diligentiae et utilitatis ratio videtur, si duplices balnearum camerae fiant, inferior caementicia et superior suspensa.'

[2] 'asseres abiegni ad lineam aut regulam aequaliter dirigantur, ne plus habeant grossitudinis quam digitos tres. hos inter se sesquipedali mensura divisos ordinabis' etc. Krohn, seeing the difficulty of 'abiegni' (especially on his own view that Faventinus is a mere hack), desperately adopts the MSS' 'abstinei' – meaning, I suppose, timbers that do not get the worm. But this word seems to be unknown in Latin; and it would remove only one of the differences between this passage and Vitruvius. One must protest at the attitude of Krohn, who, determined to see in Faventinus a mere hack (which he is not), will strike out or alter when he can any sign of Faventinus' independence. See further my remarks in the Commentary.

[3] 'postea primo manu inducatur impensa pumicea, et trullizetur ut canna subigatur, deinde harena et calce dirigatur. tertio marmor tunsum super calce inducatur et poliatur.'

He even makes provision for a coffered soffit, if you desire a more refined type of vault.[1]

Once more, then, Faventinus writes with extensive additional knowledge of vaulting technique, gained presumably by builders under the Empire in the great age of concrete. But the passage contains another clue to his date, in its use of the words 'grossior' and 'grossitudo'. These have an air of the fourth century at the earliest.

Turning to Palladius, we find that Book 1 Chapter 13 contains an abbreviated version of Faventinus. The spacing and material of the poles – *lignum Gallicum*, or firwood[2] – the material of the chains suspending them from the truss, the method of infilling with reed bundles and the use of pumice for the first coat, of sand-mortar and powdered marble for the other two are all repeated. On the other hand, Palladius omits the prescription for coffering. As we shall see, he intends these vaults only for inelegant rooms. But at this point I must notice an apparent exception to the conclusions of Nohl, which until now have worked so well. In this passage, for once, Palladius seems closer to Vitruvius than to Faventinus; for he says 'Asseres ligni Gallici vel cupressi directos et aequales constituemus', whereas Faventinus had omitted and Vitruvius had recommended cypresses. This, however, is mere coincidence. It is Palladius' own insertion, presumably inspired by contemporary practice. Unlike Vitruvius, he believes both timbers equally suitable. In fact, while most of the chapter is from Faventinus, the introduction is Palladius' own. 'It will be more useful', he begins, 'to make the vaulted rooms in our rustic buildings from materials easily found on the property. So we shall make them either of boards or reeds, in the following fashion. We shall place straight and equal poles of firwood, or cypress where the vault is to be'[3] – and at this point he begins

---

[1] 'si quid autem urbanius cameris addere volueris, fasciculos de canna facies et laquearis operis vel delicatae aut arcuatilis camerae exemplis uteris' (I prefer 'aut' to the 'ut' of the MSS).

[2] See above, p. 6.

[3] 'Cameras in agrestibus aedificiis et ea materia utilius erit formare quae facile invenietur in villa. Itaque aut tabulis faciemus, aut cannis, hoc genere. Asseres ligni Gallici vel cupressi directos et aequales constituemus in eo loco ubi camera facienda est', etc. Note the use of 'villa' to mean apparently the whole property, an interesting expansion of the word; also the self-sufficiency after which Palladius strives.

his epitome of Faventinus. These vaults of boards, suggesting garden-temples of the eighteenth century, are not to be found in Vitruvius. They reappear in greater detail in I, 40, describing the vaults of baths. In neither place is there any manuscript support for Barth's emendation, at first sight attractive, of 'tubulis' for 'tabulis'. One recalls late Roman vaults of amphorae and other hollow ingredients. But the context in Palladius makes planks more natural. As, in I, 13, planks are an alternative to bundles of reeds, so in the bigger vaults of I, 40, they are an alternative to real concrete – 'camerae in balneis ligninae fortiores sunt. Quae vero de tabulis fiunt, virgis ferreis transversis et ferreis arcubus sustinentur.' Or, rejecting the tabulae, one can place on the system of rods and arches a set of tied wands held together by matted clay and hair. Below (either the planks or the tied wands, one presumes) you are to spread the *structura testacea*.[1]

Palladius, then, adds nothing to concrete vaulting technique. He takes over Faventinus' prescriptions, and yet leads us to think that he would not often use them, but something rather more rustic. So, once again, we seem to catch a picture of building in the later fourth century, when concrete was used as a last resort. The same picture, I think, will result, if we examine Palladius' remarks in I, 10 on pit sand and the other ingredients of concrete. But his relation to Faventinus here has been much disputed; and the topic deserves a special appendix.

On the water-supply, the later authors differ, not for the better, from Vitruvius, who retains much Hellenistic science and recalls the precise and accurate piping of cities such as Pergamum. The virtues of this part of Vitruvius are not recognized by such writers as R. J. Forbes,[2] and therefore need some scrutiny.

Vitruvius describes contemporary methods of supplying water in Book VIII, Chapter 7 (Rose 206–10). One can quote here only the main heads of his account and his differences from Faventinus and Palladius. There are three ways, he tells us, of conveying water – in channels of masonry, lead pipes, or earthenware con-

---

[1] 'Sed si tabulas nolis imponere, super arcus ac virgas bipedas constitues ferreis ancoris colligatas, capillo inter se atque argilla subacta cohaerentes, et ita impensam testaceam subter induces.'

[2] *Studies in Ancient Technology*, I, pp. 160–1 (on the North Aqueduct of Pergamum, which, like Vitruvius' lead and earthenware waterpipes, runs happily up and down hill).

duits.[1] If in channels, the masonry is to be solid and the gradient not less than $\frac{1}{4}$ inch in 100 feet.[2] Arch over the channel with masonry ('structura confornicetur'), so that the sun cannot reach it. Where the channel reaches the city, build a *castellum*, with a triple distribution tank and three outlets through pipes (*fistulae*), one to public pools and fountains, one to public baths and one for supplying private needs. The third, in times of drought, can be turned off at the head in favour of the public supplies. If there are hills between the spring and the city, tunnel through them. Take the water through the living rock or tufa, where that is present; whereas earth or sand is to be lined with walls and vaults ('parietes cum camera in specu struantur'). Here, then, we have Vitruvius describing the typical Roman aqueduct that we all know, with slight gradients and ponderous masonry channels.

But (iv) if we use lead pipes, we follow a different method – Fig. 4, (*a*) and (*b*). We start with a *castellum* at the spring; for it seems that according to Vitruvius, one is always needed where there are to be outlet pipes. We build another *castellum* at the entrance to the city, and connect the two structures by a set of lead pipes (*fistulae*). Each stretch of pipe is to be at least 10 foot long.[3] Vitruvius then explains the sizes and names of different pipes. The course of the pipes, he then continues, can cross small depressions on substructures and circumvent the larger. But if the depression is a continuous valley, then one runs the pipes down into it. Along its floor, one gives them a low substructure, to keep their course as level as possible. Then, when it comes to the upward slope on the other side, the water in the pipes will gently swell and flow uphill.[4] If there is no level *venter* built across the valley but only a knee-joint (*geniculum*) where the gradient changes, the water will burst out. And even along the *venter* itself we must contrive small valves to relieve air pressure in the

---

[1] 'rivi per canales structiles, aut fistulis plumbeis, seu tubulis fictilibus, quorum hae sunt rationes.'

[2] 'rivi libramenta habeant fastigata ne minus in centenos pedes sicilico.' Pliny (*N.H.* 31, 57) bears out the reading 'sicilico' (quarter-inch) as the smallest slope practicable in 100 feet. So all editors, including even Krohn, read it here, though some manuscripts, including G and H, read 'semipede'.

[3] Contrast the lengths of only 4 foot in the aqueduct at Pergamum (Forbes, *Ancient Technology, loc. cit.*).

[4] 'leniter tumescit et exprimitur in altitudinem summi clivi.'

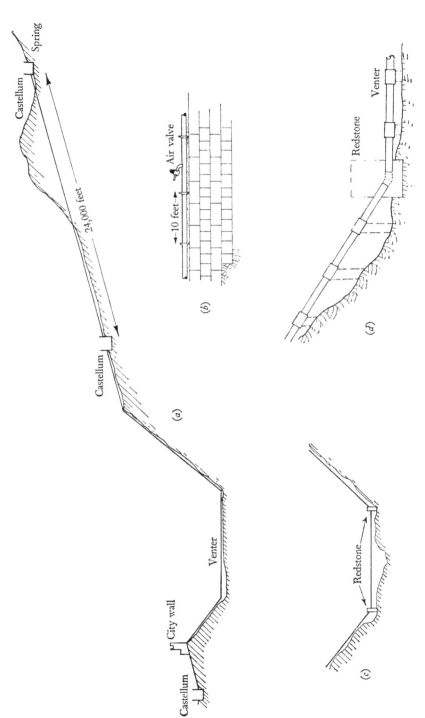

Fig. 4. Vitruvius' aqueducts for lead and clay pipes: (a) aqueduct for lead pipes, with detail of *venter* (b); (c) *venter* of aqueduct for clay pipes, with detail of 'elbow.' (d)

pipes.[1] One is amazed at the technical refinement of all this; and one must surely see in it a good example of Hellenistic hydraulics. After all, has not Vitruvius quoted only a few paragraphs before (Rose 206, 9) the dictum of Archimedes that any stretch of so-called level water on the surface of the earth forms part of a sphere, its centre at the centre of the earth? Vitruvius concludes his section on aqueducts of this type by recommending *castella* at intervals of 24,000 foot (200 *actus*, or nearly 5 miles), but nowhere in the depressions, only on the line of the continuous overall slope ('neque omnino in vallibus sed in perpetua aequalitate'). These are not for water-storage like the intermediate reservoirs in Faventinus and Palladius, but strictly to limit the effect of breakages and to aid repairs.[2]

Vitruvius associates a third, cheaper kind of aqueduct with clay pipes – Fig. 4, (*c*) and (*d*); and it is not quite clear how much, or how little substructure he recommends for it, though he says that in general it is to be built like the lead aqueduct.[3] The wall of the clay pipes is to be not less than 2 fingers thick, and each section of pipe is to have a tongue at one end, to give tight joints, which are to be caulked with a mixture of quicklime and oil. At the two changes of gradient, between the descent and the *venter* and

[1] 'etiam in ventre colliquiaria sunt facienda, per quae vis spiritus relaxetur.' Gundermann's 'colliquiaria' seems obviously right, as against the 'colliviaria' of the manuscripts. Granger translates the whole of this passage to suggest a long V-shaped curve stretching right across the valley, with a long series of angles, none of them sharp – none, in fact, a *geniculus*. I have followed Morgan, and I think that Granger's version, though plausible, will not fit. It is true that Vitruvius says (Rose, 208) there must be no great change of angle (*geniculus*) in the valley. But he also says that across the foot of the valley there is to be no high substructure, but that the course should be level for as far as possible ('ut sit libramentum quam longissimum'), while on the next page (Rose, 209, 15), while presupposing an almost identical course for an aqueduct of clay pipes, he talks of the last pipe of the descent, the first of the horizontal course and the first of the ascent as 'ex decursu tubulus novissimus', 'primus librati ventris' and 'primus expressionis', the upward slope being called the 'expressio', because, after the long horizontal stretch, when it comes to the opposite slope the water gently wells up, 'ut exprimatur in altitudinem summi clivi'. What Vitruvius is recommending is an aqueduct that does not prolong the slopes of the hills, however gently, to the middle of the valley (forming a 'geniculus' there), but that boldly descends the natural slopes to the valley floor. This in fact happens with the Roman aqueduct of Pergamum (F. Graeber, *Wasserleitungen von Pergamon* (Berlin 1888), Pl. 2). Finally, Vitruvius is careless in his use of *geniculus*, for, after saying there shall be none, he speaks of two, one at each end of the horizontal stretch (*venter*), in the aqueduct for earthenware pipes.
[2] 'ut si quando vitium aliqui locus fecerit, non totum omneque opus contundatur et in quibus locis sit factum facilius inveniatur.'
[3] 'reliqua omnia uti fistulis plumbeis ita sunt conlocanda.'

between the *venter* and the ascent, the joints must be set tightly in a hole pierced through a standing block of red stone.[1] The violent blasts of air often arising in water-pipes will by these means be given no chance to form. Finally, arrange that the water, when it first enters the aqueduct, carries ashes through the pipes, thus blocking all remaining leaks. Clay pipes, concludes Vitruvius, are healthy, and have the advantage that any one can mend them. Leadworkers even look unhealthy; while earthenware is preferred for meals even by the owners of silver services, because of the relish it adds. Thus far Vitruvius, who seems to be recommending a very economical aqueduct of the Pergamene type.

At Pergamum, as is well known, the stones of the Hellenistic aqueduct, which rested on the ground, were replaced in the end by a Roman arched structure across the lower part of the valley, which gave the building in its last phase a *venter* resembling Virtuvius'. But what instances of a *venter* are known in western aqueducts? Almost all are laid out in one continuous and very gentle slope, often raised high above valleys and plains.

But Faventinus seems to show a decline in skill from the run of Roman aqueducts, let alone the Hellenistic. His sixth chapter seems to keep the general Vitruvian picture, but he does add wooden channels ('canalibus ligneis'), rather surprisingly, to Vitruvius' three alternatives. In aqueducts of masonry he requires a fall of $1\frac{1}{2}$ foot in a stretch of 60 or 100 foot, and positively demands a violent rush of water; and in all this he is enthusiastically repeated by Palladius.[2] Such gradients make us think of Granada rather than Classical Rome. Faventinus continues that, if there are intervening hills, we are to tunnel through them along the line of the overall slope ('ad libramentum capitis aquae'). After this, he becomes brief and yet tortuous. For instance, it is hard to tell whether his wooden pipes or channels are to take the water in the tunnels or in a course skirting the mountain in the open air. (See the commentary, below.) For

---

[1] 'lapis est ex saxo rubro in ipso geniculo conlocandus' (set up at the angle itself) 'isque perterebratus, uti ex decursu tubulus novissimus in lapide coagmentetur et primus etiam librati ventris' – and the same principle for the other change of gradient.

[2] According to Faventinus, 'pede semis inter centenos vel LX pedes structura submittatur, ut animata aqua non pigro impetu decurrat'; and according to Palladius (LX, 11), 'si per planum veniet, inter sexagenos vel centenos pedes sensim reclinetur structura in sesquipedem, ut vim possit habere currendi.'

crossing valleys, he certainly recommends arches of the normal
Roman type as one way to take the water ('structura solida vel
arcuatili ad libramentum aquae occurratur'); but does he imply
as an alternative a system like Vitruvius' *ventres?* He may,
perhaps, by his words 'aut fistulis plumbeis aut canalibus libere
cursus dirigatur'.[1] He then advises the builder to take a long,
winding course, where the spring is very high and the force of the
fall needs to be broken. Like Vitruvius, he recommends earthenware pipes for health and cheapness. But his pipes are more rustic
than Vitruvius'. They have no tongues, but are to grow narrower
from one end ('ex una parte angustiores fiant') presumably taper-
ing like the tiles on a Laconian roof; and the smaller end is to
penetrate its neighbour by one palm. If so, of course, the pipes
would be far from watertight. So it should not surprise us that
Faventinus' aqueduct should cometimes cease to flow – because,
according to him, the springs sometimes dry up. So it will be
useful, he says, to build reservoirs (*conceptacula*) along the route,
which will not dry up, even if the spring does.[2] On the whole
Faventinus' passage on water-supply, though perhaps fairly
practical, lacks the precise Hellenism of Vitruvius. One feels that
he really envisages only the simplest water-channels. After all, he
is prescribing only for second-rate canals to private properties;
whereas Vitruvius, according to the testimony of Frontinus himself (1, 25) may have been one of the most influential water-men
of his age.[3]

[1] The manuscripts appear to read 'libre'. Rose reads 'libere', Krohn 'librate'. If Krohn
were right, we should surely have to suppose that the lead pipes, too, were raised to the
line of the gradient ('ad libramentum aquae'), whereas the advantage of lead pipes, in
Vitruvius at least, was that they could depart from it. Palladius, too (see below) seems to
have believed that the lead pipes could wander up and down. So I prefer 'libere'. 'Librate'
in the sense that water was to find its own level at the nodal points, would have needed
further words of qualification and explanation.

[2] 'non alienum videtur etiam conceptacula' (not a Vitruvian word) 'locis opportunis
facere, ut si aquae exhaustae solis ardoribus fuerint aut venas sitiens terra consumpserit,
nihilominus de aquis aqua ministretur.'

[3] It is hard to evaluate this passage. Frontinus (1, 25) gives two different traditions,
that the adjutage called the quinarius was invented by Agrippa or that it was brought into
use 'a plumbariis per Vitruvium architectum in usum urbis exclusis prioribus'. Frontinus
rejects the reason given for the name by this tradition, that the pipe was made out of a
strip of lead five digits wide.
  This is the reason for the name that Vitruvius himself gives in his eighth book (Rose
208). Is Frontinus saying that the man or the book induced the water-men to adopt this
size? Uncharacteristic imprecision in Frontinus!

Palladius IX, 11 seems simple and clearly written after Faventinus, but modifies little of his information. He, too, recommends four kinds of conveyance for the water; and also that, crossing a flat stretch of country, the water should have Faventinus' downward slope of 1½ foot in a stretch of 60 to 100 foot. We shall either tunnel through an intervening hill or run the channel obliquely along its sides.[1] If a valley interposes itself, we shall raise the channel on pillars or arches up to the proper level, or we shall shut it in leaden pipes and allow it to take a downward course, and to rise on the other side of the valley.[2] It is striking to find him applying so clearly at this late date the Vitruvian principle that water will find its own level. But he nowhere uses the tell-tale Vitruvian word, *venter*. And when he goes on to describe the healthier pipes of earthenware, he knows nothing of Vitruvius' 'tongued joints', but gives their walls Faventinus' thickness of two fingers, and specifies, like him, that it is vital for it to run into its neighbour for the distance of one palm. The application of lime and oil, to plug all leaks, will follow as a matter of course. Finally, and again varying Faventinus' argument, he says that a careful man will also build reservoirs, so that even a poor piping system may supply him with plenty of water.[3]

Unlike their accounts of concrete, but as we should rather expect, the prescriptions of Faventinus and Palladius for the water-supply mark no real advance on Vitruvius. But it is interesting that they should contrive and manipulate such a rush of water. Though they do not tell us so much, we may feel that at the back of their minds was the habit, growing under the later Empire, of using water-power where one could.

Nothing in this long survey has really shaken Nohl's conclusion, that Palladius is the latest of these three writers. As a working hypothesis, it has served us well; and it has helped us, I hope, to reach a tentative conclusion, that Faventinus wrote his compendium while skilled work in concrete was still taken for granted,

---

[1] 'aut per latera eius aquam ducemus obliquam, aut ad aquae caput speluncas librabimus, per quarum structuram perveniat.'

[2] 'Sed si se vallis interserat, erectas pilas vel arcus usque ad aquae iusta vestigia construemus, aut plumbeis fistulis clausam deiici patiemur, et explicata valle consurgere.'

[3] 'Diligentioris erit aquarum receptacula fabricari, ut copiam vel inops vena procuret.'

but in an age which all the other evidence from the vocabulary to the programmes discussed would mark as late – say the early fourth century. Palladius was a gentleman, wrote good Latin and used helpful authorities for his manual on the running of a typical estate of the late Empire. Some of his sources are very respectable, though we cannot always name them, and his information on the proportions of foundations apparently goes back to the world of Greek architecture. But he writes after the great age of concrete, and when materials are beginning to come into use which we regard as somewhat medieval. Nor is it an accident that, in successively organizing Vitruvian material, these two Latin and apparently western writers should confine themselves to private houses, while the 'praestans sapientia' appropriate to public architecture, to which Faventinus at the end almost appeals to come forward and write, should not have been forthcoming. The fourth century was an age of private architecture. Constantius, half-way through it, could still at a pinch transport and erect obelisks, but found the glory of Trajan's Forum altogether beyond the reach of emulation.[1] Again, whatever the interest or knowledge which earlier Imperial architects may have shared with Vitruvius in the matter of detailed proportion and appropriate ornament, we find no one in the fourth century, Faventinus, Palladius or the architects of houses or basilicas, any longer capable of training their sensibilities along lines so precise and refined. The only Vitruvian proportions specifically retained by both writers are those for hot bathrooms – which have a utilitarian reason,[2] and those for oblong rooms in houses, that the height should be half the combined length and breadth. Even this last proportion is not purely aesthetic, as anyone will know who has spent the hot season beside the Mediterranean; and it is given

[1] 'Verum cum ad Traiani forum venisset, singularem sub omni caelo structuram . . . haerebat adtonitus per giganteos contextus circumferens mentem nec relatu effabiles nec rursus mortalibus adpetendos. Omni itaque spe huius modi quicquam conandi depulsa', etc. (Ammianus xvi, 10, xv, on the visit of Constantius to Rome in AD 356).

[2] Vitruvius (v, 10: Rose 126) says that their width should be two-thirds of their length, but gives no reason. Faventinus (16: Rose 300, 14) repeats the proportion, adding that the heat of the fire will draw better with this shape ('melius enim ignis per angustiora latitudinis cellarum operabitur' – another instance of Faventinus' rather helpless Latin). Palladius (1, 40) repeats the proportion, and gives Faventinus' reason in a more correct version. 'Cellae autem sic disponantur, ut quadrae non sint: fortius enim vapor inter angusta luctabitur.' An oblong room creates a draught for the steam.

with more care in Vitruvius than in his two successors. For whereas he himself tells us that dining-rooms should be a double square on plan, and that all oblong rooms (*conclavia*) should have a height half the combined length and breadth, while 'exedrae' and square rooms should have a height one-and-a-half times their breadth,[1] Faventinus 15 drops the prescription for the planning of dining-rooms, and Palladius drops all mention of *exedrae* and square rooms, and prescribes the Vitruvian height for dining-rooms and bedrooms only.[2] So the rule of proportion is petering out in these writers, just as it seems, from actual buildings, to have begun to peter out in the reign of Diocletian. In Ostia in the fourth century there seems to have been little regard for the Orders or for any clearly marked proportions.

This brings me to my last point. Herbert Koch remarked, in the downright German fashion, that Vitruvius' book had no effect whatever on the architecture of Early Imperial Rome.[3] Be that as it may – and I hope to investigate the claim one day – his influence on architectural writing, even before the collapse of the Empire, is by no means negligible. Composing a useful manual for domestic architects and their private clients, Faventinus finds Vitruvius the most convenient, perhaps the only substantial written source, and one which needs, on the whole, to be brought up to date surprisingly little. Whatever the backwardness of his style and, at times, his construction in the view of sumptuous emperors and architects, in the kind of building science which, until very recently, our own architectural students acquired from Mitchell's *Building Construction*, Vitruvius' material still seemed valuable, even indispensable, centuries later. The amount of it retained and the parts of it rejected can surely tell us a great deal about the state of ordinary Roman building in the time of Faventinus, which I have put about AD 300, and even more, perhaps, of its progress and recession by the time of Palladius, whom I should place, very tentatively, about a century later.

---

[1] Vitruvius VI, 4, viii (Rose 143, 3).

[2] 'Mensura vero haec servanda est in tricliniis atque cubiculis, ut quanta latitudo et longitudo fuerit, in unum computetur, et eius medietas in altitudinem conferatur' (Palladius I, 12).

[3] In the introduction to his treatise *Vom Nachleben des Vitruv* (Baden Baden 1951).

APPENDIX: THE INGREDIENTS OF THE BEST CONCRETE

The sequence Vitruvius, Faventinus, Palladius and the further conclusion that I have drawn, that of these three writers Faventinus marks the most developed stage of Roman concrete, seem to me virtually established by all the topics that I have raised in the preceding essay. But I cannot deny that on one subject, the actual composition and preparation of concrete, various difficulties arise, most of which I cannot readily explain. I must now set them out, hoping that a technical expert in this field will put me right.

Even here, for the most part, Faventinus 8 repeats Vitruvius II, 4, while Palladius I, 10 keeps close to Faventinus. But, especially in the introductions to these passages, the three authors differ in rather puzzling ways.

All three commend 'pit sand' (*harena fossicia*) as normally the best for a load-bearing wall (*structura*) of concrete, and insist that it have no earthiness about it (as tested by the sound it makes between one's fingers and its failure to stain a white cloth). But whereas Vitruvius says 'genera autem harenae fossiciae sunt haec, nigra, cana, rubra, carbunculus', Faventinus says definitely 'Harenae fossiciae genera sunt tria; nigra, rubra, carbunculus' – which seems strange, because he omits the gray pit-sands, which, according to Miss Blake,[1] contained many varieties, while retaining the carbunculus, which according to her 'has little value as a building material and was never imported into Rome'.[2] Palladius agrees that there are only three sorts of pit-sand, but makes these the black, the gray and the red ('genera sunt tria, nigra, cana, rufa'), and then continues, rather surprisingly, to list them in order of merit. 'Omnium praecipue rufa melior: meriti sequentis est cana: tertium locum nigra possidet.' But according to Ashby their relative merit was already familiar to the Augustans. On p. 32 of his *Architecture in Ancient Rome* (London 1927), he remarks that the discovery then 'of the red variety (far superior

---

[1] *Ancient Building Construction*, I, p. 43.

[2] *Ancient Building Construction*, p. 44. She offers no evidence. She is probably relying, as often hereabouts, upon notes of van Deman. And she contradicts Vitruvius, who calls it 'egregia in structuris' (II, 6, vi; Rose 44).

to the gray in use previous to the time of Augustus) was an important factor in the development of brick-faced concrete'. Why, then, should Palladius (less well-versed, as I have argued, than Faventinus in the niceties of concrete construction) be the first to stress its merit?

I cannot begin to solve these problems. Possibly the carbunculus, the colour of cinders,[1] or coals, and therefore admitting a wide range of tints, could be identified by Faventinus with some of the *harenae canae*, from which in Vitruvius' time, when a greater range of gray sands was used, it was carefully distinguished. Faventinus' *rubra* and *carbunculus* would then correspond to the *rufa* and *cana* of Palladius. There seems to be nothing in Faventinus' third chapter (listing *sabulo masculus*, *harena* and *carbunculus*) to contradict this view, which seems at least possible.

Where pit-sand is lacking, continues Vitruvius, use the sand from river-beds or gravel-beds, or even the seashore. But sand of this sort (I follow Morgan in taking Vitruvius' 'ea' to apply to all three kinds of sand) has the drawback that it takes a long time to dry, so that one can build it up only at intervals, while it will never support a vault ('neque concamerationes recipit'). Furthermore, the salt in concrete made from sea-sand will dissolve any coat of stucco applied to it. But pit-sands quickly dry, and concrete made from them will support a coat of stucco and also a vault without any trouble – provided, of course, that they are not exposed, once they are dug up, to the action of sun and moon and frost, which will reduce them to earthiness.

It is interesting that Vitruvius says that pit-sands set easily, and should imply that one can erect whole structures of them without interruption. If pozzuolana takes a long time to set – and though one has often been told this, the standard textbooks seem remarkably reticent on the subject – then it cannot be identified with Vitruvius' 'pit-sand', for all the pleading of Miss Blake. Nor were the Romans, if they used 'pit-sand', compelled by their slow-setting concrete to construct their vast structural armatures of piers and arches, so well attested in existing Imperial buildings.

Faventinus mentions sea-sand, river-sand and the sand from gravel-beds as alternatives to the pit-sands, but attributes to sea-

[1] 'In Etruria excocta materia efficitur carbunculus' (Vitruvius II, 6, vi; Rose 44).

sand alone the slow setting and structural weakness which Vitruvius had seen in all three. This is only apparent carelessness. For he repeats Vitruvius' remark just afterwards that river-sands are too tenuous for proper concrete ('fluviaticae propter macritatem signino operi incongruentes sunt'), and rightly considered this sufficient condemnation of them. Moreover, he sees sun and rain as the ruin of exposed pit-sand – more likely agents than Vitruvius' moon and frost. Palladius can only follow him in all this, and departs from him only at the very end, to say that exposed pit-sand is spoilt by sun, frost and rain.

Discussion of the next topic, how to pick the best sand for stucco, is puzzling, and involves a crux. Vitruvius remarks that river-sand is too tenuous for proper concrete, but that 'baculorum subactionibus in tectorio recipit soliditatem'. The reading 'baculorum', accepted both here and in VII, 3, vii (Rose 168) by Rose and by Lewis and Short, is very uncertain. Faventinus 8, according to Rose himself, reads 'iaculorum'. Krohn reads 'liaculorum' both in Vitruvius and Faventinus. This word is supposed to mean a 'smoother' or 'polisher', the Greek λειαντήρ. But the connection seems fragile and ill-attested, although, according to Middleton,[1] the Romans did apply plaster to walls with a wooden float, exactly as is done nowadays. It would be reasonable to beat the plaster on to walls. Or Vitruvius may mean that it is well beaten before its application. For according to VII, 3, x (Rose 169) Greek stuccadores 'etiam mortario conlocato, calce et harena ibi confusa, decuria hominum inducta, ligneis vectibus pisunt materiam, et ita ad certamen subacta tunc utuntur' – 'construct a mortar-trough (as Morgan translates the passage), mix the lime and sand in it, bring on a gang of men, and beat the stuff with wooden beetles, and do not use it until it has been thus vigorously worked'. So, on balance, I prefer the 'baculorum' of the older editions to the 'liaculorum' of Krohn and Granger.

At this point in the discussion Palladius (and only he) adds the sensible advice that one should soak the salt out of the sea sand.

Turning to the lime in the concrete, one finds the most specific advice in Faventinus, who here justifies my general picture of him. Vitruvius says that it is made by burning 'white stone' (the

---

[1] In the *Encyclopædia Britannica* (9th Edition), *s.v.* 'Rome', p. 810, n.s.

hard carboniferous limestone so common around the Mediterranean?) or *silex* (a word which the Ancients could apply to many
sorts of hard stone – cf. Blake, *Ancient Building Construction*, p.
40). The denser, harder stone will provide lime for *structura*, the
more porous for stucco. Faventinus, eschewing the vague term,
silex, prescribes that 'calx itaque de albo saxo aut tiburtino aut
columbino fluviatili coquatur aut rubro aut spongia' – that lime
be made from white stone, or travertine (chippings one supposes),
or dove-gray river-stone, or red stone or porous stone. Large
blocks of *saxum rubrum* were used, as we saw, by Vitruvius for
supporting and enclosing the joints in his earthenware aqueduct
where it changed its gradient. It is traditionally said to come from
the Grotta Rossa quarry, near Veii. In any case, Faventinus
speaks with knowledge; and Palladius adds only one other stone,
marble.[1] This is interesting. Either he is speaking as an habitué of
the marble coastline of Luna, *en route* for Gaul, or for Corsica and
Sardinia: or he is already condoning the Late Antique and
Medieval practice of pillaging derelict Classical buildings.[2]

Finally, Vitruvius prescribes the proportions of sand and lime
to be mixed; three of sand to one of lime, if it is pit-sand; only two
of sand, if it is river-sand. But Faventinus and Palladius after him
prescribe two of sand in all cases. All alike recommend the
strengthening of mortar from river-sand by the addition of a
third part of crushed earthenware.

With this our authors end their discussion of this fundamental
topic. It adds far less than we might have hoped to our knowledge
of this branch of later Roman building science. But, if we examine
their treatment narrowly and directly, at least it need not upset the
conclusions at which we have already arrived.

---

[1] 'aut rubro, aut spongia, aut marmore.'
[2] This is of a piece with his advice in Book VII, I (considered very significant by K. D.
White on p. 31 of his *Roman Farming*), that we prepare our threshing-floor by pressing
it with a round stone or a fragment of broken column.

M. CETI FAVENTINI
DE DIVERSIS FABRICIS
ARCHITECTONICAE

In the Text of Valentine Rose's Large Edition

(1867)

De artis architectonicae peritia multa oratione Vitruvius Polio aliique auctores scientissime scripsere. verum ne longa eorum disertaque facundia humilioribus ingeniis alienum faceret studium, pauca ex his mediocri licet sermone privatis usibus ornare fuit consilium. quae partes itaque caeli et regiones ventorum salubres aedificiis videantur et qua subtilitate nocivi flatus avertantur aditusque ianuarum et lumina fenestris utiliter tribuantur, quibusve mensuris aedificiorum membra disponantur, quibus signis tenuis abundansque aqua inveniatur, alia etiam quae aedificandi gratia scire oportet brevi succinctaque narratione cognosces.

Vitr. 1, 2.
Primo ergo quae principia ad architecturam pertinere debeant studiose attendere convenit. omnia enim pulchro decore ac venusta utilitate fieri poterunt, si ante huius artis peritus ordo discatur. nam architecturae partes sunt octo, quae sunt ordinatio, dispositio, venustas, mensura, distributio, aedificatio, conlocatio, machinatio. ex his Graeci quinque vocabulis studium architecturae esse docuerunt. nam ordinationem ταξιν, dispositionem διαθεσιν, venustatem et decorem εὐρυθμιαν, modulorum mensuras συμμετριαν, distributionem οἰκονομιαν appellaverunt. ordinatio est ergo membrorum dispositio, et constat ex quantitate, quam Graeci ποσοτητα vocant. quantitas est modus singulorum membrorum universo respondens operi. dispositio est apta rebus conclavium institutio, et operis futuri forma tribus figuris divisa, quae a Graecis ἰδεα appellatur. haec sunt ergo tres figurae, ichnographia, orthographia, scenographia. ichnographia est areae vel soli et fundamentorum descriptio. orthographia est laterum et altitudinis extructio. scenographia est frontis et totius operis per picturam ostensio.

On proficiency in the art of architecture Vitruvius Pollio has written eloquently and at length, and other authors with extraordinary knowledge. But for fear that their lengthy and erudite copiousness may frighten less aspiring intellects off these studies, I have taken the resolution to clothe in everyday language a few items from their works, to be of use for private needs. So, if you wish to know what exposures to the sky and the winds would seem to result in healthy buildings, what skills will keep out harmful breezes, and ensure easy entrance through the doors and workable lighting from the windows, or what are the right measurements for the parts of a building, or what are the signs of a meagre or an abundant water-supply – if, in short, you are inquiring into anything that you need to know when you propose some building, you will find it in this treatise, briefly and succinctly told.

First then you must take careful notice of the principles Vitr. 1, 2. that are proper to architecture. For a beautiful order and a pleasing usefulness will have the chance to result everywhere, if the principles of the art are learnt beforehand, in the order approved by experts. For architecture comprises eight parts – order, disposition, beauty, measurement, distribution, building, siting and mechanical engineering. The Greeks taught that the study of architecture embraced five of these. For they called order *taxis*, disposition *diathesis*, beauty and elegance *eurhythmia*, the measurement of units *symmetria* and distribution *oeconomia*. Order then is the disposition of the members of a building, and consists of quantity, which the Greeks call *posotes*. Quantity is the manner in which the single members of a building respond to the effect of the whole work. Disposition is the apt arrangement of rooms to their uses, and also the design of the building that is to arise, shown in figures of three different kinds, called by the Greeks *ideas*. These, then, amount to the three sorts of figure called the plan, the elevation and the perspective. The elevation is the setting out of the proposed side walls and height. The perspective is the display of the façade and the whole building with the help of painting.

Ferunt quidam philosophorum Eratosthenen mathemati-
cis rationibus et geometricis methodis aequinoctiali tempore
per gnomonicas umbras orbis terrae spatia esse metitum et
sic certos ventorum didicisse flatus. tenere ergo orientem
aequinoctialem ⟨subsolanum, meridiem austrum, occidentem aequinoctialem⟩ favonium, ⟨septentriones⟩ septentrionem. inter ceteros tamen Andronicus Cyrrestes cum octo
ventis orbem terrae regi adseverasset, exempli causa Athenis
turrim marmoream octagonam instituit, in qua imagines
ventorum sculptas contra suos cuiusque flatus ordinavit,
supraque ipsam turrim metam marmoream posuit et
Tritonem aeneum conlocavit et ita est modulatus ut cum
ventus aliquis adspirasset quodam momento in gyro
ageretur et supra caput eius resisteret et dextera manu
virgam tenens ipsum esse flantem monstraret. itaque esse
inter subsolanum et austrum ad orientem hibernum eurum,
inter austrum et favonium ad occidentem hibernum africum,
inter favonium et septentrionem chaurum, quem quidam
corum vocant, inter septentrionem et subsolanum aquilonem. hoc modo et nomina et partes et numeros ventorum
scire coeptum est. sed plerique duodecim ventos esse
adseverant, ut est in urbe Roma Triton aeneus cum totidem
thoracibus ventorum factus ad templi Andronici Cyrrestae
similitudinem. supra caput venti virgam tenens eundem esse
flantem ostendit. observabis ergo ne ianuas aut fenestras
contra nocivos flatus facias. nocivi enim sunt flatus ubi aut
nimis incumbunt aut acerrima frigora faciunt, ut et homines
et animalia laedant. frigorosis ergo regionibus a meridie aut
ab occasu hiberno ianuas et fenestras facies, aestuosis vero a
borea et septentrione fieri ordinabis.

Now some philosophers say that Eratosthenes, using 2. On winds. mathematical arguments and geometrical methods, measured the extent of the globe of the earth at the time of the equinox from the shadows cast by gnomons, and that he thus learnt the fixed directions for the course of the winds. Thus due (equinoctial) east is the quarter for *subsolanus*, the south for *auster*, due west for *favonius*, and the north for *septentrio*. But Andronicus Cyrrhestes, among others, maintained that the globe of the earth was under the sway of eight winds, and to show this erected an octagonal tower of marble at Athens, on which he placed carved reliefs of the winds, each to face its own quarter. Above the tower he placed a marble pinnacle and upon this a bronze Triton, and so arranged it that when a wind struck it with any force it would turn and stay firm above the relief of the wind, while the rod that it held in its right hand indicated that this was the very wind now blowing. So it could be shown that, between *subsolanus* and *auster*, *eurus* blows from where the sun rises in winter, and *africus* from where it sets in winter, between *auster* and *favonius*; *chaurus* (called by some people *corus*) between *favonius* and *septentrio*, and *aquilo* between *septentrio* and *subsolanus*. In this way people began to recognize the number and names of the winds. But most men assert that there are twelve winds, exemplified at Rome by the bronze triton above a pedestal of twelve faces, each showing a wind, made after the pattern of Andronicus Cyrrhestes' prototype.[1] It holds its rod above the head of the wind on the pedestal, and shows that this is the wind now blowing.

You must take care, then, not to make doors or windows that face harmful winds. For winds do harm either when they are too strong or when they bring cold so bitter, that it harms men and animals. So in cold districts you must place your doors and windows so that they face the south or the direction of winter sunsets, while in hot districts you must contrive that they face the north and *septentrio*.

[1] Reading the *exempli* of S for the *templi* of Rose and all earlier editors.

3. De aquae
inventione.
Vitr. VIII, 1
(Pall. IX, 8).

Quoniam usibus omnium maxime necessariae aquae videntur, primo quae genera terrae tenues aut abundantes venas emittant, quibus etiam signis altius depressae inveniantur, quomodo ex fontibus vel puteis ducantur, quae nocivos aut salubres habeant liquores, studiose scire oportet. aquae ergo fontanae aut sponte profluunt aut saepe de puteis abundant. quibus tales copiae non erunt, signis infra scriptis quaerenda sunt sub terra capita aquarum et proxima fontibus altiora puteis colligenda. ante solis itaque ortum in locis quibus aqua quaeritur aequaliter in terra procumbatur et mento deposito per ea prospiciatur. mox videbis in quibuscumque locis aqua lateat umores in aera supra terram crispantes et in modum tenuis nebulae rorem spargentes, quod in siccis et aridis locis fieri non potest. quaerentibus ergo aquam diligenter erit considerandum quales terrae sint. certa enim genera sunt in quibus aut abundans aut tenuis aqua nascatur. in creta tenuis et exilis nec optimi saporis invenitur, in sabulone soluto tenuis, limosa et insuavis altioribus locis mersa. in terra nigra stillarum umores exiles magis ex hibernis liquoribus collecti saporis optimi spissis et solidis locis subsidentes. glareae vero mediocres et incertas venas habent sed egregia suavitate. in sabulone masculo et harena et carbunculo certiores et salubriores et abundantiores sunt copiae aquarum. in rubro saxo et copiosae et bonae inveniuntur, sed providendum erit ne inter rimas saxorum quoniam suspensae sunt decurrant. sub radicibus montium et in saxis silicibus uberiores et salubriores et frigidiores aquae inveniuntur. campestribus autem fontibus salsae et graves et tepidae et non suaves erunt, sed si sapor bonus invenitur, scito eas de montibus sub terra venire in medios campos, ibique umbris arborum contectae praestabunt montanorum fontium suavitatem.

3. On finding water.

Since water seems to be what everyone most needs for all purposes, we must study to find out first of all what kinds of soil supply us with meagre or abundant springs, what signs too we have that these can be struck further below the surface, how their supplies are conveyed from fountains or wells, and which provide harmful or healthy water. Now springs of water often gush up of their own accord; or they can often bubble up from wells. People who do not enjoy such plenty must use the clues that I give below to trace springs of water below ground, and they must collect in wells the water to be found lower down not far from springs. So in the places where you are looking for water you must lie level and prone on the earth before sunrise, and with your chin let down on to the ground you must look around you. Soon you will see in the places where water lies concealed the wisps of vapour rising into the air and scattering dew like fine clouds. This would be impossible on parched, dry land. So when you are looking for water you should consider the nature of the soils. The kinds which give either abundant or meagre supplies run true to form. The water found in chalk is meagre and poor and not of the best savour. In loose sand it is meagre and muddy; and deeper down it is foul. In black soil tiny drops, mostly from the winter rains, collect and sink into hard, firm places, and have an excellent savour. Gravels contain smallish, unpredictable springs; but the water is beautifully sweet. In coarse sand, ordinary sand and *carbunculus* the supply of water is more reliable, healthier and more abundant. In red stone copious amounts of good quality are found; but one must take care that they do not run away, since they are locked in fissures of the stone. Richer, healthier and cooler water is found at the foot of mountains, among hard shiny stones. But in springs on the plain supplies will be salty, heavy, lukewarm and far from sweet. If springs of a pleasant savour are found, you can be sure their water has run underground from the mountains into the midst of the plain, and that there, shaded by the branches of trees, it will display the sweetness of a mountain spring.

45

Signa autem investigandae aquae alia huiusmodi invenientur, tenuis iuncus, salix erratica, alnus, vitex, harundo,
hedera, alia quoque quae sine umore nasci non possunt.
quoniam autem in lacunis similia nascuntur, facile his
credendum non est. itaque sic inventiones aquae probabis.
fodiatur ergo ubi haec signa fuerint inventa, ne minus in
latitudinem pedes iii, in altitudinem pedes v, et circa solis
occasum vas plumbeum aut aeneum mundum intrinsecus
perunctum oleo in imam fossuram inversum conlocetur,
supraque fossuram frondibus vel harundinibus missis terra
inducatur. item alia die aperiatur, et si sudores aut stillae in
vaso invenientur, is locus sine dubitatione aquam habebit.
item si vas ex creta siccum non coctum eadem ratione
positum et opertum fuerit, si is locus aquam habebit, alio die
vas umore solutum invenietur. vellus lanae similiter in eo
loco positum si tantum umoris collegerit ut alia die exprimi
possit, magnam copiam aquae locum habere significat.
lucerna plena oleo incensa si in eodem loco similiter adoperta
in alia die lucens fuerit inventa, indicabit eum locum aquam
habere, propterea quod omnis calor ad se trahit umorem.
item in eodem loco si focum feceris et vaporata terra umidum
nebulosumque fumum suscitaverit, ostendit locum aquam
habere. cum haec ita fuerint reperta certis signis, in altitudinem putei defodiendi erunt quousque caput aquae
inveniatur aut si plura fuerint in unum colligantur. maxime
tamen sub radicibus montium in regione septentrionali signa
aquae sunt quaerenda. in his enim locis suaves et salubres et
abundantiores inveniuntur, quoniam naturae beneficio a
solis cursu separantur et arborum aut montium umbris
velatae frigida gratia aestate, hiberno tepida suavitate
profluent.

But there exist other tell-tale signs of this sort, when we are looking for water – the slender rush, the wild willow, the alder, the *agnus castus*, the reed, the ivy and all other plants that cannot spring up without water. But since plants of this sort also spring up in hollows temporarily damp, you must not trust them too readily. So this is how you will prove that water can be found. Where you find these tell-tale plants, dig a hole not less than 3 foot wide and 5 foot deep, and around sunset place a clean vessel of lead or bronze, greased inside with olive oil, upside down in the bottom of the hole. Cover the hole with rushes or leafy sprays, and put earth on top of these. Wait a day or two to uncover it. Then if the inside of the vase shows sweating or drops of water, without a doubt this place will yield water. Again, if a dry vessel of unbaked white clay is similarly placed and covered over, then, if the ground will yield water here, the vessel will be found some days later dissolved by the damp. Similarly, if a woollen fleece is laid in this spot and collects enough moisture to be wrung out some days later, it shows that the ground here contains a great quantity of water. If a lamp full of oil is lit and similarly buried at this place, and if on another day it is found still alight, then it will show that the ground here contains water; for all heat draws water to itself. Again, if you build a fire on the same spot and if the earth that it warms renders the rising smoke damp and misty, then it shows that the place contains water.

So when this presence has been discovered by sure signs, you must dig wells into the depth of the earth until you find a spring of water or until, if there are several, they are collected at one point. You should make your most intensive search for signs of water at the foot of mountains in localities with a northward aspect. For the springs found at these spots are sweet and healthy and more copious. For nature is kind to them, keeping them out of the sun's way; while, shaded by trees and mountains, their streams will possess a refreshing coolness in summer, a pleasant, moderate warmth in winter.

4. De puteorum
fossionibus et
structuris.
Vitr. VIII, 7.
(Pall. IX, 9).

In puteorum autem fossionibus diligenter est cavendum
ne fodientibus periculum fiat, quoniam ex terra sulphur
alumen et bitumen nascitur, quae res cum in se convenerint
pestiferos spiritus emittunt. et primo occupatis naribus tetro
odore reprimunt animas corporibus, et si non inde cito
fugerint celerius moriuntur. hoc autem malum ubicumque
fuerit hac ratione vitabis. lucerna accensa in eo loco demittatur. quae si ardens remanserit sine periculo descendes. quod
si ereptum ei lumen fuerit, cavendum erit ne in eo loco
descendatur. sed si alio loco aqua non invenietur, dextra ac
sinistra usque ad libramentum aquae putei fodiantur et per
structuram foramina quasi nares intus in puteum demittan-
tur, qua nocivus spiritus evaporet. sed cum aqua inventa
fuerit, signinis operibus parietes struantur ita ne venarum
capita excludantur. in signinis autem operibus haec servare
debebis. primo ut harena aspera paretur et caementum de
silice vel lapide toficio calcisque proxime extinctae duae
partes ad quinque harenae mortario misceantur. puteum
ergo fodere debebis latum pedibus octo, ut a binis pedibus
structura in circuitu surgat et quattuor cavo relinquat.
structuram vero cum facere coeperis, vectibus ligneis
densabis sic ut nitorem frontis non laedas. sic enim solidata
structura adversus umorem fortior erit. quod si limosa aqua
fuerit, salem ei miscebis et sua virtute sapores mutabit. sed
licet auctores ad quinque partes harenae duas partes calcis
mitti docuerint, isdem mensuris et redivivas expensas fieri
monstraverint, melius tamen inventum est ut ad duas

But in digging wells you must take special care that your 4. The digging
workmen are exposed to no danger. For sulphur, alumen and lining of
and bitumen occur in the earth; and when they meet one wells.
another they emit poisonous exhalations. These first attack
the nostrils with a foul smell and then prevent the body from
breathing, so that, if one does not escape quickly one soon
dies. Wherever this danger arises, you can avoid it by the
following means. Light a lamp and let it down into the
place. If it stays alight, you can quite safely descend. But if
the flame is snuffed out, then take care not to go down there.
However, if there is a dry place adjacent, let wells be dug on
the right and left down to the level of the spring, and then
through their masonry-lined walls let vents like nostrils
be pierced, leading to the original well between them,
vents through which its poisonous air can evaporate.[1] Once
water has been found, line the walls with brickwork, in
such a way that the actual springs are not shut off from
the well.

Now for structures of baked brick you must observe the
following precepts. First that rough sand is obtained and
aggregate of shiny black stone or tufa, and that two parts of
lime lately burnt be mixed with five of the sand in the
mixing-trough. Then you will need to dig a well 8 foot in
diameter, so that a brick lining 2 foot thick can be built from
the bottom upwards and leave 4 foot clear in the middle.
When you begin to build this lining, ram it home tight with
wooden rams in such a way that you don't damage the gloss
of its face. For in this way the lining will be solidified, and
more resistant to damp. But if the water is muddy, add salt
to it, and by its virtue this will change the flavour.

But although authors have prescribed that two parts of
lime should be blended with five of sand, they have also
shown that if you observe these proportions, you will incur
renewed expenses later.[2] But a better mixture was found, of
two of sand to one of lime; so that a greater initial expendi-

---

[1] For once, Faventinus is long and clumsy, compared with Vitruvius (VIII, 6;
Rose, 213). But his meaning seems the same.

[2] Reading 'monstraverunt'. See Introduction, p. 19, n. 3.

harenae una calcis misceatur, quo pinguior inpensa fortius caementa ligaret. similiter et in testaceis operibus facies. puteum autem cum fodere coeperis, si terra solida non fuerit aut harena rubrica aut sabulo fluidus aut exsudans umor fossionem resolvet, tabulas axium directas fodiendo submittes et eas vectibus ligneis transversis distinebis, ne labens terra ruina ponderis periculum fodientibus faciat.

5. De utilitate
aquae probanda.
Vitr. VIII, 5
(Pall. IX, 10).

Quoniam ergo ante omnia aquae usus necessarius habetur, his experimentis utilitas eius probanda erit. itaque si naturaliter fontes profluent, considerandum erit prius quales homines et quam salubri corpore circa eos fontes habitent. itaque si corporibus valentibus, cruribus non vitiosis, coloribus nitidis, non lippientibus oculis, purgatos salubresque fontes probabis. quod si novi fontes aut putei fossi fuerint, aquam eximes, in vas aeneum nitidum sparges, et si maculam non fecerit optime probabilis erit. missa etiam in vaso aeneo nitido si decocta fuerit et limum vel harenam in fundo non reliquerit, legumen in ea si cito coquatur, bona erit. non minus si perlucidi fontes fuerint et sine musco aut quibusdam inquinamentis, salubrem perpetuamque aquam futuram significabit.

6. De aquae
inductione.
Vitr. VIII, 7
(Pall. IX, 11).

Ductus autem aquae quattuor generibus fiunt, aut forma structili aut fistulis plumbeis aut tubis vel canalibus ligneis aut tubis fictilibus. si per formam aqua ducitur, structura eius diligenter solidari debet, ne per rimas pereat. canaliculus formae iuxta magnitudinem aquae dirigatur. si planus locus fuerit, infra caput aquae structura conlocetur et, si longior planitia fuerit, pede semis inter centenos vel LX pedes structura submittatur, ut animata aqua non pigro impetu decurrat. nam si intervalla montium fuerint, ad libramentum

ture might bind the aggregate more firmly. You shall act in a similar way with all building of brickwork.[1]

But when you begin to dig your well, if the earth is not solid, and if the excavation is wrecked either by the slipping of fine sand[2] or the flow of coarse sand or the sweating of moisture, then as you dig you must let down straight vertical planks and hold them apart by wooden cross-bars. This will prevent the slipping of the earth and save your diggers from the danger of its weight.

Now since we reckon that we need the use of water more than anything else, we must prove the worth of our springs by the following experiments. So if the springs are already flowing of their own accord, we shall first have to ask ourselves what sort of men they are and how healthy they are who live around them. And so, if their bodies are healthy, their legs not deformed, their complexion bright, their eyes not bleared, you can approve the springs as clean and salubrious. But if the springs are fresh or the wells newly dug, then you must take some of the water and sprinkle it on a clean bronze vessel. If it makes no mark, it will be of high quality. Also if, when poured into a bronze vessel and boiled away, it leaves no mud or sand at the bottom, and if green vegetables cook quickly in it, then it will be good water. No less obviously, if the springs are very clear and contain no moss or other weeds, this will show that the water is healthy and will never dry up.

5. Proofs that a particular supply of water can be used.

Now there are four ways of conveying water; an enclosure of masonry, lead pipes, pipes or channels of wood, or pipes of earthenware. If the water is conveyed through masonry, this must be carefully built into a total mass, so that no cracks will afford a leakage. The channel inside the aqueduct must be arranged according to the current of the water. If the neighbourhood is flat, the building must be at a lower level than the spring, and if the plain is a broad one, the building must be lowered at the rate of $1\frac{1}{2}$ foot in every 100, or even in every 60 foot. This will put life into the

6. The conveyance of water.

---

[1] Inserting 'omnibus'. See Commentary.
[2] Reading 'harena lubrica' for 'harena rubrica'.

capitis aquae specus sub terra erit structura aut roboreis canalibus aquae ductus componatur. quod si concavae vallium demissiones inpedient, structura solida vel arcuatili ad libramentum aquae occurratur, aut fistulis plumbeis aut canalibus libere cursus dirigatur. verum si altior locus fuerit unde aqua ducitur, aliquanto inferius planitia inflexa libretur, ut veniens aqua fracto impetu lenius decurrat. aut si longius de monte ducitur, saepius flexuosas planities facies. minori etiam sumptu et utilius tubis fictilibus inducitur. cum a figulo ergo fient, ne minus duorum digitorum grossitudine corium habeant. sed ipsi tubuli ex una parte angustiores fiant, ut alter in alterum per ordinem vel palmum ingrediantur. iuncturae autem eorum calce viva oleo subacta inliniantur. et antequam a capite aqua demittatur, favilla per eos cum parvo liquore laxetur, ut si qua vitia tubuli habuerint excludantur. salubrior etiam multo tubulorum materia invenitur. ex plumbo enim cerussa nascitur, quae corporibus humanis nociva est. exemplum autem huius plumbariorum deformitas probat, qui tractando plumbum exsucati sanguine foedo pallore mutantur. nam cum fere omnes structas vasorum argenteorum vel aeneorum habeant mensas, tamen propter saporis integritatem fictilibus vasculis utuntur. non alienum videtur etiam conceptacula locis oportunis facere, ut si aquae exhaustae solis ardoribus fuerint aut venas sitiens terra consumpserit, nihilominus de receptaculis aqua ministretur. canalium vero et tubulorum ligneorum facilis et usitata aquae inductio videtur.

7. De mensuris et pondere fistularum.
Vitr. VIII, 7
(Pall. IX, 12).

Fistulae ergo plumbeae pro magnitudine aquae hanc soliditatem et mensuram accipere debebunt. si centenariae fundentur denum pedum, M et CC libras fusurae accipiant.

stream and give it a brisk flow. If hills interrupt the course
of the water, build a masonry tunnel underground along the
line of flow from the spring, or arrange to take the water in
channels of oakwood round the obstacle.[1] But if cross-
valleys interrupt the desired flow, you must build up to it,
using solid masonry or an arched structure, or else allow the
water to find its own level in lead pipes or channels. But if
the spring is situated high up, then rather below it you must
arrange a winding channel, all on one level, so as to break
the force of the descending stream. If the course is a long
one from the hill, you will construct a good many of these
flat winding stretches. It will cost you less, too, and be more
practical if you bring the water in earthenware pipes. When
made of earthenware, pipes should have an outer wall not
less than 2 fingers thick. But each stretch of pipe must be
narrower at one end, so that one may slip into another, each
in succession, for a distance of one palm. The actual joints
are to be lined with a mixture of quicklime and oil; and
before the water is let in from the spring, ashes in a little
fluid are to be released through them, to stop any faults in
the pipes.

Earthenware is found to be a much healthier material for
water-pipes. For lead gives rise to white-lead, which is
hurtful to the human body. One example which proves the
point is the deformity of plumbers. From their dealings with
lead they acquire a dreadful anaemic pallor. While almost
everybody has tables equipped with vessels of silver or
bronze, yet people actually use earthenware vessels because
they preserve the flavour of the dishes.

It evidently helps, too, to make little reservoirs at suitable
points. Then, if the streams are dried up by the heat of the
sun or the springs drunk up by the thirsty earth, water can
still be fetched for our use from these reservoirs.

The conveyance of water in wooden channels and pipes
is clearly an easy and common method.

Now lead pipes will be made of the following weights and
measures according to the amount of water. 'Hundred-

7. On the weights
and measures of
water-pipes.

[1] See the Commentary.

octogenariae denum pedum, DCCCCLX libras accipiant. quinquagenariae denum pedum, DC libras accipiant. quadragenariae denum pedum, CCCCLXXX libras. tricenariae X pedum, CCCLX libras. vicenariae X pedum, CCXL libras. octonariae C libras.

8. De harenae
natura probanda.
Vitr. II, 4
(Pall. I, 10).

Harenae fossiciae genera sunt tria, nigra, rubra, carbunculus. ex his quae manu comprehensa stridorem fecerit, optima et purgata erit. quae autem terrosa fuerit, non habebit asperitatem. etiamque in vestimentum candidum si miseris et effusa si nihil sordis reliquerit, idonea erit. si vero non fuerit unde harenae fodiantur, tunc de fluminibus aut de glareis excernenda erit aut de litore marino. sed marina harena in structuris hoc vitium habet, tarde siccat. unde onerari se continenter non patitur. nisi intermissionibus requieverit opus, pondere gravata structura rumpetur. cameris etiam salsum umorem remittendo tectorium opus saepe resolvit. fossiciae vero celeriter siccescunt et tectoria non laedunt et concamerationes utiliter obligant. sed fossiciae recentes statim in structuras mitti debent. fortius enim comprehendunt caementa. nam si sub sole diutius fuerint aut imbribus pruinisque solutae, et terrosae et evanidae fiunt. fossiciae itaque cum recentes sunt, tectorio operi propter pinguedinem non conveniunt. fluviaticae autem propter macritatem signino operi incongruentes sunt, sed iaculorum subactionibus in tectorio opere recipiunt soliditatem. in caementicias autem structuras pura harena mittatur.

9. De calcis
utilitate probanda.
Vitr. II, 5
(Pall. I, 10).

Calx itaque de albo saxo vel tiburtino aut columbino fluviatili coquatur aut rubro aut spongia. quae enim erit ex spisso et duro saxo, utiliter structuris conveniet. quae autem ex fistuloso aut exiliore lapide fuerit, conveniet operi tectorio. in commixtione ad duas partes harenae una calcis mittatur. in fluviatili autem harena si tertiam partem testae cretae addideris, miram soliditatem operis praestabit.

pipes' 10 foot long will need 1200 *lb.* of cast metal, 'eighty-pipes' of this length 960 *lb.*, 'fifty-pipes' 600 *lb.*, 'forty-pipes' 480 *lb.*, 'thirty-pipes' 360 *lb.*, 'twenty-pipes' 240 *lb.* and 'eight-pipes' 100 *lb.*

There are three kinds of pit sand – black, red and ashen.[1] Of these the sand that grates harshly when gripped in the hand will be of high quality and pure. Earthy sand will have no roughness. Again, if you hurl sand against a white cloth and it falls away without leaving a stain, it will be good sand. If you have no pits from which to dig your sand, then you are to strain it from rivers or gravel-beds, or from the sea-shore. But sea sand has this fault when used in buildings; it is slow to dry out, and cannot bear a load immediately after laying. Unless the work is interrupted at various stages and given a rest, the structure will be broken by its own weight. Moreover in vaults it often ruins plasterwork by emitting salty moisture. But pit sands quickly dry, do not hurt plasterwork and act as a bonding to complicated vaults. But pit sands must be used in buildings while still freshly dug. For then they bind the aggregate more firmly. For if they are long exposed to the sun or are loosened by rain or frost, they become earthy and etiolated. As a corollary, when pit sands are freshly dug, they are too rich to be suitable for plasterwork. But river sands, because of their leanness, are unsuitable as mortar in brickwork, but if they are thoroughly pounded by sticks they become strong enough for plaster work. But let pure sand be used for building works.

8. Testing the quality of sand.

As for lime, let that be burnt from white stone or travertine or dove-grey river-stone, or Grotta Rossa or sponge-stone. The lime that is made of close-grained hard stone will be very useful in building-works. But the lime from porous or lighter stone will be suitable for plasterwork. At the mixing let one part of lime be added to two of sand. But if to the river sand you add a third part of powdered earthenware, it will give the work an unbelievable solidity.

9. Testing the utility of lime.

[1] For the Latin term, 'carbunculus', see my appendix on the ingredients of the best concrete.

10. De late ribus faciendis.
Vitr. II, 3
(Pall. VI, 12).

Faciendi autem lateres sunt ex terra alba vel creta vel rubrica aut sabulone masculo. haec genera terrae propter levitatem fortiora sunt operi. cetera genera quoniam aut gravia sunt aut paleas non continent aut umore sparsa cito solventur, propterea fabricis inutilia videntur. ducendi autem sunt lateres verno tempore, ut ex lento siccescant. qui enim solstitiali tempore parantur, vitiosi fiunt, quoniam calor solis torridus corium in summo cito desiccat, et quasi integri videntur, postea umor interius dum siccatur contrahit frontes et scissuris dividit et inutiles operi lateres facit. maxime tamen tectorio operi inutiles erunt, si ante biennium inducantur. non enim possunt ante penitus siccari. fiunt autem laterum genera tria. unum quod graece Lydium appellatur, longum sesquipede latum pede, quo nostri utuntur. sunt et alia duo laterum genera, unum πενταδωρον et alterum τετραδωρον. δωρον autem Graeci palmum appellant. itaque artifices quinque palmorum publica opera extruere consuerunt et IIII privatorum. fieri debebunt et semilateria remissas quae laterum iuncturas interposita reparent. ita enim fiet ut cum alter alterius protegit coniunctionem, firma structurae soliditas surgat.

11. De parietibus la tericiis tectorio operi parandis.
Vitr. II, 8
(Pall. I, 11).

Laterici parietes tribus inductionibus prius solidentur, ut opus tectorium sine vitio accipiant. nam si recentes structurae et inductiones fuerint et non ante siccaverint, cum arescere coeperint, scissuris venustatem operis corrumpent. in urbe autem propter multitudinem hominum parietes caementicii altius struuntur, ne latius soli magnitudinem occupent. merito ergo latericiam habere non potuit, ne pondere cito corrupta fabrica laberetur. latericiis ergo parietibus vitia quae solent accidere ne fiant, hoc modo erit providendum. in summitate parietum structura testacea cum

But your sun-dried bricks you are to make out of white earth or chalk or ruddle or coarse sand. Because of their lightness these kinds of earth are stronger in a structure. The other sorts, either because they are heavy or don't hold straw or quickly dissolve when damp, are clearly useless in building works. You are to cut your bricks in the spring, so that they may dry slowly. Those that are made at midsummer become defective. For the intense heat of the sun quickly dries the outer skin. They look like sound bricks; but later the centres dry and contract and pull in the outside, making cracks and rendering them useless. They will be of no use at all for plaster finishes, if used before two years are out. For they cannot dry thoroughly in less time. 10. How to make sun-dried bricks.

Now there are three kinds of sun-dried brick. The first is called in Greek the *Lydian*, and it is 1½ foot long, 1 foot wide. It is the brick that our people use. Of the two other sorts, one is called *pentadoron*, the other *tetradoron*. The Greeks call the palm of the hand *doron*. So contractors have become accustomed to making public buildings of five-palm bricks, private of four-palm. Half-bricks, too, will have to be made. For these will be inserted to end the series of staggered joints, which is needed so that one brick will cover the joint made by another, and thus ensure that a solid structure is erected.

Let walls of sun-dried brick be treated to three coats of plaster. They will then be solid enough to take stucco-work without trouble. If both walls and plaster-coats are new and have not dried out, they will crack when they begin to dry and thus ruin the beauty of the work. But in Rome, because of the enormous population, concrete walls are reared high in the air, so that buildings may not cover a large area. So it was only reasonable that Rome could have no walls of sun-dried brick, thus avoiding building-work that quickly collapses under its own weight. So if you want to avoid the faults that habitually develop in walls of sun-dried brick, you must take the following precaution. On the top of your walls erect a coping of baked earthenware with projecting cornices. It is to be 1½ foot in height. Then, even if your 11. On preparing brick walls for their final coats.

prominentibus coronis altitudine sesquipedali extruatur, ut si corruptae tegulae aut imbrices erunt, parietes tamen solidi permaneant.

12. De generibus arborum et utilitate caesionis. Vitr. II, 9 (Pall. XII, 15).

Materies arborum quae ad utilitatem fabricae parabitur, autumni tempore antequam favonii flare incipiant utiliter caeditur. prius tamen usque ad medullam securibus circumcisae stantes intermittantur, ut inutilis umor decurrat et venarum raritas exsiccata solidetur. sed genera arborum has inter se vires et differentias habent. abies ergo habens aeris plurimum et ignis, minimum terreni et umoris, merito non est ponderosa et naturali rigore non cito flectitur a pondere. laricis vero materia in omni fabrica maximas habet utilitates, primo quod ex ea adfixae tabulae subgrundae ignis violentiam prohibent, neque enim flammam recipiunt neque carbonem faciunt. larix vero a castello Laricino est dicta. quercus terrenis satietatibus abundans parum habens umoris, cum in terrenis operibus obruitur perpetuam servat utilitatem. cuius apta aedificiis materies et in umore posita perpetuam exhibet utilitatem. fagus quod aequalem habet mixtionem umoris et ignis, in umore cito marcescit, siccis locis utilis est. populus alba et nigra, salix et tilia ignis et aeris habent satietatem, in fabrica utiles, in sculpturis gratae inveniuntur. alnus, qui proximus aquae nascitur, tener et mollis materia extra aquam fabricae inutilis est, sed hoc mirum in se habet quod in umore palationes spisse defixae structuram supra se factam sine vitio servant. ulmus et fraxinus in omni opere cito flectuntur, sed cum aruerint rigidae sunt, lentoris causa catenis utiles. carpinus in omni opere tractabilis et utilis invenitur. cupressus et pinus admirandas habent virtutes, quod non cito pondere curvantur, durant enim integrae semper. cedrus si umore non corrumpatur, eandem habet virtutem. sed quomodo de pino resina decurrit, sic et ex ea oleum quod cedrium dicitur.

tiles or shingles become defective, your walls will still remain firm.

Timber that is to be of any use in building is conveniently cut in the autumn, before the west winds begin to blow. Previously, however, the trees should be cut as far as the pithy core and then left to stand, so that the useless sap can run down and the finer veins become dry and solid. But the various kinds of trees have the following strong points and distinguishing characteristics. The silver fir, with the greatest amount of air and fire, the least of earth and water, as a natural consequence is light and of an inborn stiffness not readily deflected by any weight. But larch timber is of the greatest usefulness in every kind of building, chiefly because larch-boards fixed under the eaves keep out the violence of fire. For they neither catch fire nor are reduced to cinders. The larch gets its name from the fort of Laricinum. The oak, abundantly rich in the element of earth but with too little water, retains its usefulness for ever when buried in earthen constructions. Its timber's general fitness for buildings is displayed by its continuing usefulness even when placed in water. The beech, because it contains equal proportions of water and fire, quickly rots in water but is useful in dry places. The black and white poplar, the willow and the lime all have more than enough fire and air. They are useful in buildings, and give pleasure in carvings. The alder, which grows very near water, is a tender and pliant timber, and is useless for building-work away from water. But it has this wonderful property, that stakes of it fixed into a close framework below water preserve any building erected upon it without fear of harm. The elm and the ash quickly warp in any structure, but when they have dried out they are stiff and make good chains because of their elasticity. The hornbeam is found to be tractable and useful in all kinds of work. The cypress and the pine have the admirable quality that they are not readily warped by loading, for they keep their firmness and shape for ever. The cedar, provided it is not rotted by damp, has the same virtue. But just as resin oozes

12. On the uses and preparation of timber.

si libri aut clusa eo inungantur, nunquam tineis aut carie solventur. multis itaque templis propter aeternitatem ex ea lacunaria sunt facta. etiam folia eius cupresso similia sunt. nascitur maxime in Creta et in Africa et in Syriae regionibus. quaecumque ergo ex parte meridiana caeduntur utiliores erunt, ex parte autem septentrionali proceriores sunt arbores sed cito vitiantur.

13. De fabrica villae rusticae disponenda. Vitr. VI, 8 (Pall. I, 21).

Primo ita cortes et culinae calidis locis designentur. bubilia in parte meridiana ita ut ad ortum aut ad focum boves spectent. nitidiorem enim cultum recipiunt, si ad lumen attendant. latitudo XV pedibus disponatur et in singulis paribus VIII pedes relinquantur. equilia calidis locis ordinentur, et obscuriora fiant ut securi equi pabulentur. ovilia et caprilia pro magnitudine agri disponantur. cella vinaria contra frigidissimas caeli plagas conlocetur. lumen fenestris a septentrione tribuatur, ut undique frigidus aer vina incolumia servet. vapore enim omnia corrumpuntur. torcular huius in septentrione ponatur. cella autem olearis in meridie constituenda est. fenestrae ab eadem parte tribuantur, ne frigore oleum cum sordibus retineatur et suavitas saporis pereat. torcular huius in meridie statuatur. magnitudo pro abundantia rei fiat. granaria ad septentrionem vel aquilonem spectent, ut aere gelidiori fruges tutius serventur. vaporatae enim regiones curculiones et alia genera bestiolarum nutriunt quae fruges corrumpunt. horrea fenilia pistrina extra villam sunt constituenda, ut ab ignis periculo villae sint tutiores. si quid vero melius et nitidius facere volueris, exempla de urbanis fabricis sumes.

14. De dispositione operis urbani. Vitr. VI, 6.

Urbani itaque operis gratiam luminosam esse oportet, praesertim cum nulli vicini parietes inpediant. disponendum

out of pine, so out of cedar there runs an oil which is called *cedrium*. If this is rubbed into books or boxes, they will never perish from grubs or decay. Therefore many temples are given ceiling-coffers of cedar, because it lasts for ever. Its leaves, too, are similar to those of cypress. It grows chiefly in Crete, Africa[1] and parts of Syria. Now whatever trees are felled in southward-facing regions are more fit for use. But those on northerly slopes are larger, but quickly decay.[2]

First site your yards and kitchens in warm spots, your stalls for oxen in a southward-facing place, and so that your oxen may face the sunrise or a fire. For they acquire a glossier complexion if they face the light. Let the width of the building be 15 foot, and allow 8 foot for single pairs. Arrange your stables in warm sites, but darken them so that your horses can feed in peace. Build pens for sheep and goats according to the area of your grazing-land. Site your wine-cellar to face the coldest quarters of the sky. Bring in light through northward-facing windows, so that cold air from all sides may preserve the wines. For they are all corrupted by hot air. The actual press is to be placed in the northern part of the cellar. *13. On siting the dependencies of a country villa.*

But the cellar for olive oil is to be placed to the south. Let it be given windows, too, on its south side, so that no cold will make dirt cling to the oil and ruin the gentle flavour of the liquid. Place the press at the southern end of the room. Let the size be governed by the amount of supplies available. Let your granaries face north or north-east, that the colder air may preserve the grain. For air from the hot quarters of the sky nourishes weevils and other sorts of animal pest that ruin the produce. Granaries, hay-lofts and bakeries are to be placed outside the farm-buildings, so that your farms may be safer from the danger of fire. If you wish to build something better and more artistic, you will take your pattern from buildings in town.

The beauty of a property in town must owe a lot to its lighting, especially when there are no adjacent walls to *14. On planning a house in town.*

[1] Presumably, the Roman province (modern Tunisia).
[2] This meaning is not immediately obvious. But see p. 5 of my Introduction.

erit tamen ante, ut certa genera aedificiorum caeli regiones apte possint spectare. hiberna ergo triclinia hibernum occidentem spectare debent, quoniam vespertino lumine opus est. nam sol occidens non solum inluminat sed propter vim caloris tepidas facit regiones. cubicula et bibliothecae ad orientem spectare debent. usus enim matutinum postulat lumen. nam quaecumque loca meridiem spectant umore vitiantur, quoniam venti umidi spirantes madidos flatus omnia pallore corrumpunt. triclinia verna et autumnalia ad orientem spectare debent, ut gratiora sint quando his uti solitum est. aestiva triclinia ad septentrionem spectare debent, quod ea regio praeter ceteras frigidior est et solstitiali tempore iocundam sanitatis voluptatem corporibus praestat.

15. De mensuris aedificiorum. Vitr. vi, 4.

Tricliniorum et conclavium quanta latitudo et longitudo fuerit in uno computata mensura, ex ea medietas altitudini tribuatur. si autem exedrae aut oeci quadrati fuerint, media pars mensurae in altitudinem struatur. pinacothecae et plumariorum officinae in parte septentrionali sunt constituendae, ut colores et purpurae sine vitio reserventur. de vaporatis enim regionibus corruptelae nascuntur.

16. De fabrica balnearum. Vitr. v, 10 (Pall. i, 40).

Balneis locus eligendus est contra occasum hibernum aut partem meridianam, ut sole decedente vaporetur usque ad vesperum quod tempus ad lavandum tributum est. suspensurae calidarum cellarum ita sunt faciendae ut primum area sesquipedalibus tegulis consternatur, inclinata ad fornacem ut pila missa intro resistere non possit sed redeat ad praefurnium. flamma enim sursum adsurgens calidiores efficit cellas. supraque laterculis bessalibus et rotundis pilae instruantur ex capillo et argilla subacta, in privato pedibus binis semis, in publico ternis. tegulae bipedales super

interrupt this. Its arrangement must be carefully drawn up beforehand, so that definite parts of the building can be given their proper aspect. Thus winter dining-rooms should face the winter sunset, for they need the evening light. For the setting sun not only gives light but gives out a heat sufficiently strong to warm that part of the sky. Bedrooms and libraries should face the east. For their use demands morning light. For any apartments that face due south are spoilt by damp. This is because damp winds breathe moisture and corrupt anything with the pallor of decay. Spring and autumn dining-rooms should face east. This will make them pleasanter at the seasons when we normally use them. Summer dining-rooms must face the north, for that region is pre-eminently the cold quarter, and at the summer-solstice it imparts to our bodies a pleasant sensation of good health.

Whatever the breadth and length of your dining-rooms and your other rooms, add the two and then, taking half this total, use it as their height. But if you have semicircular recesses or rooms of square plan, let half their width be added to it to give their height.[1] Picture-galleries and embroiderers' workshops are to be placed on the north, so that their colours and purple dyes can be kept without deteriorating. For the causes of decay arise in heated places.

15. On the proportions of rooms.

You must choose a place for your bathing suite facing the winter sunset or the south, so that the sun as it goes down will heat it right up to the evening hour, the time assigned to bathing. The hollow floors of the hot bathrooms are to be so constructed that first the ground is covered with tiles $1\frac{1}{2}$ foot square and is given a downward slope towards the furnace so pronounced that when you throw a ball on to it this cannot fail to fall back into the furnace entrance. By these means the flame of the furnace rises and makes the bathrooms hotter. Above this, pillars are to be made of bricks 8 inches across and circular on plan, with a coating of hair and clay. These are to be $2\frac{1}{2}$ foot high in private bathrooms,

16. On bath-buildings.

[1] Not clear from Faventinus' Latin, but clear from Vitruvius VI, 5 (Rose 143, 8) – 'latitudinis dimidia addita altitudines educantur'.

constituantur quae pavimentum dirigant. plumbeum vas
quod patenam aeream habet, supra fornacem conlocetur,
alterum simile frigidarium secus, ut quantum caldae ex eo in
solio admittatur tantum frigidae infundatur. magnitudines
autem balnearum pro hominum copia aut voluntatis gratia
fieri debebunt, dummodo cellae sic disponantur ut quanta
longitudo fuerit tertia dempta latitudo disponatur. melius
enim ignis per angustiora latitudinis cellarum operabitur.
lumen fenestris aut hibernis aut meridianis partibus tribuatur.
aestivis balneis hypocausteria pro loci magnitudine cum
piscinis in septentrione vel aquilone constituantur, et ab
eadem parte maxime lumen fenestris admittatur, ut salubri-
orem et corporibus iocundiorem gratiam praestet. in villa
rustica balneum culinae coniungatur, ut facilius a rusticis
ministerium exhiberi possit.

17. De cameris
balnearum.
Vitr. v, 10
(Pall. I, 40).

Camerae structiles fortiores erunt. figulinae autem ad
contignationem suspendantur ita ut catenis ancoratis fixae
tegulae velut palliola quae cameram circinent sustineant.
eadem ratione et planas cameras facies. utilius autem dis-
ponetur, si regulae vel arcus ferrei fiant, ut uncis ferreis ad
contignationem suspendantur ita ut tegularum iuncturae
super regulas vel arcus recumbant. superiores ergo iuncturae
ex capillo et argilla subacta linantur. inferior autem pars
iuncturae quae ad pavimentum spectabit primo calce cum
testa temperata trullizetur, deinde albario sive tectorio opere
inducatur. maior tamen et diligentiae et utilitatis ratio
videtur, si duplices balnearum camerae fiant, inferior

3 foot in public. Tiles 2 foot square are to be laid above them, and these will set the line of the pavement. Place a lead vessel, which stands on a bronze platter, above the furnace; and stand another, similar, beside the cold bath, so that as much water as reaches the bath hot from the first vessel may come pouring into it cold. The sizes of your bath-buildings will have to depend upon the numbers and preferences of their users, always provided that the rooms are given a particular shape, their breadth being two-thirds of their length. For the heat of the furnace will carry more easily along rooms the narrow way. Light should be admitted through windows either on the wintry or on the southern side. In baths for summer use the furnaces and swimming pools, their size dependent on the area of the site, should be placed on the north or north-east, and most of the light should be admitted through windows on the same side. This will give the bathers a healthier and pleasanter refreshment. In your country farm let the baths adjoin the kitchen, so that your country-slaves can more easily wait upon you.

Vaults of masonry will be stronger.[1] But if of earthenware, let them be suspended from the roof-truss in such a way that their earthenware tiles, attached to firmly anchored ties,[2] may hold up like a small mantle the vaults that they round off. You will follow the same method in making flat vaults. But the arrangement will be more practical if there are straight bars or arches of iron, and they are suspended from the roof-truss by iron hooks, so that the joints of the tiles fall over the bars or the arches. Then let the upper faces of the joints be smeared with a coating of hair and clay. But let their lower face, which is visible from the pavement, have first a coat, laid on with the trowel, of lime and specially prepared earthenware chippings, and then a covering of whitewash or plaster. But a greater regard will seem to have been paid to good workmanship and practicality, if the vaults of bathrooms are made double, the lower of concrete,

17. On the vaulting of bathrooms.

---

[1] For this very difficult chapter, see Introduction, pp. 22ff.
[2] These need not be of metal. For the word, 'catena', is used of chains of ash in Chapter 12.

caementicia et superior suspensa. inter duas enim cameras umor retentus numquam vitiabit contignationes. sudationes etiam praestabuntur meliores.

18. De expolitionibus pavimentorum. Vitr. vii, 1.

Considerandum erit ut solum firmum sit et aequale, tunc rudus inducatur et vectibus ligneis contusum calcetur. supra inpensa testacea crassior inducatur et iterum vectibus contusa solidetur. tertio nucleus id est inpensa mollior inducatur, et politionibus insistat ne rimas inutiles operi relinquat.

19. De pavimentis supra contignationem faciendis. Vitr. vii, 1 (Pall. i, 9).

in contignationibus diligenter respiciendum est ut aequalitas soli dirigatur. item danda est opera ne axes quercei cum aesculinis commisceantur. nam quercus cum accepto umore siccescere coeperit arcuatur et rimas inutiles operi efficiet, aesculus diligenter composita ad perpetuitatem durabit. verum si inopia loci aesculus defuerit, in tenuissimos axes quercus secetur, et primum in directo iactatis axibus, sequentibus in transverso stratis, binis clavis crebro ad contignationem confixis utiliter operi subicientur. de cerro aut fago seu farno coaxationes haut ad vetustatem poterunt permanere. iactatis in ordinem et compositis axibus filix aut paleae aequaliter supersternantur, ut calcis umor ad axes pervenire non possit. tunc insuper statuminentur saxo ne minori quam quod possit manum implere. statuminibus ruderi seu novo sive redivivo ad duas partes una calcis misceatur. rudus est maiores lapides contusi cum calce mixti. inpensa crassior induci debebit ne minus crassitudine digitos

the upper a suspended vault. For the damp trapped between the two vaults will never spoil the wooden framework above. The sweating rooms, moreover, will be better so.

Make a point of seeing that the foundation (under your floors[1]) is firm and even. Then lay on the rubble, and pound it into firmness with wooden poles. Spread a thicker layer of the earthenware above it, and again pound this with rods. As your third layer spread the 'nucleus' – that is, a quantity of softer materials, and let it settle down under polishing so that it leaves no cracks harmful to the work. 18. On the polishing of pavements.

In pavements upon wooden frameworks you are to take care that the footing is level. Again, you are to take care that no rods of oak are to be included among those of winter oak. For once the oak has become damp and begins to dry out it warps, and will cause cracks harmful to the work. But the winter oak, once carefully made up into a frame, will last for ever. However, if winter oak is altogether absent because the locality is so poor in trees, let an ordinary oak be cut into the slenderest poles possible. Then, if you lay them first along the length of the floor and afterwards a second series across it, and if you drive pairs of nails frequently into the resulting frame, they will form a practical foundation for your pavement. Frames made of Turkey oak or beech or ash will not last into old age. Once your poles are placed in order and fastened together, spread above them an even course of bracken or straw, to ensure that the moisture of the lime does not reach the poles. Then weigh this down above with a layer of loose rubble made up of stones each able or more than able to fill a hand. When this support of loose rubble has been laid,[2] let lime be mixed with a rubble of freshly used or reused stones, in the proportion of one of lime to two of rubble. Rubble proper consists of the pounded fragments of larger stones, which are then mixed with lime. You should spread a thick layer 19. On laying pavements above a wooden framework.

---

[1] Not in the Latin. I have argued in my commentary from these very chapters, that Faventinus did not have the chapter-headings that now appear in his MSS. On the other hand, the abruptness of this chapter without some heading shows, I suppose, that he must have had some.

[2] Assuming that 'iactatis' or 'positis' has dropped out after 'statuminibus'.

VI. exacto pavimento ad regulam et libellam supra inpensa
testacea mollior inducatur et siccet. tum aut marmor sectile
aut tesserae aut scutula aut trigona aut favi superinponantur,
et usque eo fricetur ut iuncturae vel anguli inter se con-
veniant, tunc erit perfecta fricatura. quod si facultas non erit
unde superfigantur, ne aut lacunae aut cumuli sint, ad
regulam fricatura extendatur et supra marmor tunsum
incernatur aut harena cum calce inducta poliatur. sub divo
maxime vitanda sunt finita pavimenta, quoniam frigore et
umore saepe corrumpuntur. sed si necessitas aut voluntas
facere hortatur, hanc operis subtilitatem servabis. missas in
ordinem tabulas et alias in transversum, sicut supra mon-
stratum est, ad tignationem configes et paleam aut filicem
super aequaliter sternes et loricabis de saxo quod manum
possit implere. super rudus pedaneum induces et vectibus
ligneis frequenter densabis, et antequam rudus siccescat,
tegulas quadratas bipedales, quae per omnia latera canaliculos
habent digitales, calce viva ex oleo temperata frontibus
tegularum qua canaliculi erunt implebis et sic iunctas supra
rudus compones, ut margines tegularum cum calce compre-
hendi possint. quae res cum siccaverit quasi unum corpus
facit et nullum ad inferiora admittet. postea nucleum sex
digitorum induces, et frequenter fricabis ne setas faciat, et
tesseram duorum aut trium digitorum latam supra inprimes
aut tabulas quammagnascumque marmoreas, ut nullo modo
fabrica vitiari possit. si quis autem diligentius facere volet,
omnibus annis ante hiemem iuncturas axium faecibus

of it – one that is at least 6 fingers deep. When you have laid out the floor to the square and the level, then a softer layer of earthenware is to be spread over it and allowed to dry. Then you can lay on this either a pavement of cut marble pieces or square tesserae, or pieces that are diamond-shaped or triangular or hexagonal. The pavement is to be rubbed together until the edges and corners of the pieces exactly meet. Then the rubbing will have reached completion.

But if there is no way of fastening these pieces on their upper surface, then, to prevent fissures or puckers, you must rub an area to the level and sprinkle pounded marble on the top, or lay on a mixture of sand and lime. You must be very careful to avoid making pavements in the open air, since they are often spoilt by cold and damp. But if you are compelled or absolutely resolved to make one, you will observe the following refinement of technique. After disposing one row of planks one way and another at right angles to them, as described above, you shall fasten them together into a framework and spread an even layer of straw or bracken upon them and protect this with a covering of stones large enough to fill a hand. Above this you are to lay rubble a foot thick and ram this down everywhere with wooden poles. Then, before the rubble is dry, you are to take tiles 2 foot square, which have grooves 1 finger wide along their sides, and insert in these grooved sides a mixture of quicklime and olive oil. Then lay the tiles in such a way over the rubble that their edges will be firmly fastened by the cement. This device, once drying is complete, makes as it were a mono-lithic floor and allows no damp to penetrate into the layers below. Next you shall lay a 'nucleus' 6 fingers thick, and rub it frequently to prevent rough raised edges,[1] and press down firmly upon it a pavement of tiles 2 or 3 fingers thick or plaques of marble as large as you like, to prevent any possible harm to the fabric of the floor. But if anyone desires to take even more trouble, every year just before winter sets in he should see that the joints of the

---

[1] Literally 'bristles'.

perungui faciat. testacea spicata tiburtina pari modo fricaturis et politionibus exerceantur.

In albario opere calcem sic probare debebis. in fossa calcem, quae multo ante tempore fuerit macerata, de ascia quasi lignum dolabis, et aciem si nusquam impegeris atque adhaerens asciae viscosa videbitur, optima erit operi albario. recenter extincta et calculosa si fuerit, dum siccescere coeperit calculi crepant et inutiles rimae operi efficientur. unde proxime extinctam in opus albarium mittere non oportet.

Camerae ergo canniciae sic erunt disponendae. asseres abiegni ad lineam aut regulam aequaliter dirigantur, ne plus habeant grossitudinis quam digitos tres. hos inter se sesquipedali mensura divisos ordinabis et catenis ad contignationem suspendes ita ut binae perticae graciliores inter eos si missae, his faciant tomices ligaturas. catenae autem parentur aut de iunipero aut oliva aut buxo aut cupresso. camerae ex harundine graeca vel palustri vel grossiori rasa et contusa sic contexantur ut fasciculi aequalis admodum grossitudinis et longitudinis ante ligentur, qui possint aequalem nitorem ostendere, ut si quam cultiorem gratiam emutare volueris, fasciculi mollioris cannae facilius flexi ducantur. postea primo manu inducatur inpensa pumicea, et trullizetur ut canna subigatur, deinde harena et calce dirigatur. tertio marmor tunsum super calce inducatur et poliatur. sic et nitore gratiam et virtutem solidam facies. si quid autem

planks[1] are oiled with wine-lees. Let herringbone pavements of travertine have similar rubbings and polishes applied to them.

In preparing white plaster you will have to test your lime as follows. Take an axe and cut, as if it were timber, the lime which has been slaked a long time previously and is now lying in a ditch. If you cannot fasten the axe-edge into it, and if it clings to the blade and is obviously viscous, it will be in the best condition for plasterwork. If it has only lately been slaked and is pebbly, then when the plaster begins to dry the pebbles crack and harmful fissures will open in the plasterwork. So you must not put newly slaked lime into a work of stucco.

20. On the testing of lime for whitewash.

Now vaults of rushes are to be erected as follows. Rods of firwood are to be arranged evenly according to a plumb-line or a square. They are not to be more than 3 fingers thick. You are to place them each 1½ foot from its neighbour, and suspend them with chains from the roof-truss in such a way that pairs of thin poles can be made to run through them and make fastening-places for knots of cord. The chains are to be made of juniper or olive or box or cypress. But the body of the vault is to be of Greek reeds, either marsh-reeds or coarser reeds, sheared and pounded together, and interwoven as follows. Reed bundles of equal thickness and length are first tied to the framework, and they can be arranged to have an even surface-brightness. In this way, if you are aiming at a more refined beauty, you can easily add curving bundles of softer reeds. After that you are first to spread on a layer of pumice with your hand, and so flatten it out with the trowel that the reeds are quite covered; and then you are to give it a precise surface with a mixture of sand and lime. In the third place you are to spread pounded marble over the lime, and polish it. So you will build a work with a pleasing glow but also one of solid structural merit. But if you want to make some more elegant addition to your

21. On rush vaults.

---

[1] Latin 'axes' – normally 'poles', but apparently meaning the same as the 'tabulae' or 'planks', a few lines above. Vitruvius, in the corresponding passage of Book VII, Chapter 1, refers to the frame of 'tabulae' as a 'coaxatio'. The frames would have to be oiled from the room below.

urbanius cameris addere volueris, fasciculos de canna facies et laquearis operis vel delicatae ut arcuatilis camerae exemplis uteris.

22. De politionibus parietum caementiciorum. Vitr. VII, 3 (Pall. I, 15).

Parietes uno corio tenui et alio grossiori si fuerint inducti et politi, macritate inpensae cito corrumpentur. exemplum huius ex speculis sumere debemus, quorum tenues lamnae falsas et deformes exprimunt imagines, solidae autem lamnae veras et suae pulchritudinis formas designant. prima ergo inductione trullizata, cum arescere coeperit, iterum ac tertio loricationes dirigantur. cum tribus coriis opus fuerit deformatum, tunc ex marmore grandi trullizationes sunt subigendae. sed ipsa species sic paretur ut ante inductiones tamdiu subigantur ut rutrum ex ea mundum levetur. inarescente inductione alterum corium subtilius inducatur, ut marmoris et candoris politionibus fundata soliditas nitidum culturae faciat decorem. omnia ergo quae diligenti studio componuntur, neque vetustatibus obsolescunt neque cum purgari coeperint gratiam coloris amittunt. umidi enim parietes cum picturis ornantur desudescent, et operi obligatus color elui non potest.

23. De opere coronario. Vitr. VII, 3.

Operi coronario subtilior inpensa necessaria est, ut amplius fricata mollius nitore gratiam faciat. observandum tamen erit ne gypsum inpensae adiungatur. siticulosa enim materia dum cito arescit, vicina coronarium opus politionibus parietum et camerarum cum superinducitur ruina corrumpit.

24. De parietibus caementiciis umidis locis solidandis. Vitr. VII, 4.

Parietes vero umidis locis sic erunt solidandi. si perpetuus umor manabit, tribus pedibus ab imo, testaceo paries vestiatur et vestitura calcetur et poliatur, ne umorem admittere possit. quod si maior umor perpetuus manabit, canaliculum brevem extrues aliquantum a pavimento altius,

vaults, you must make up little bundles of reed and follow the patterns of coffered work or of refined vaulting, as, for instance, that decorated with patterns of arcs.

If walls are covered with one narrow coat and then a thicker one, and are then polished, they will soon begin to decay owing to the thinness of their coating. We should take mirrors as an example of the same thing. When their plating is thin they give false and distorted reflections, whereas solid plating gives reflections that are true, and have a beauty of their own. So when you have laid on your first coat with the trowel, wait for it to begin to dry, and then lay on a second and a third protective covering. When you have shaped up the work with three coats, then you are to apply with the trowel quantities of large marble grains.[1] A material of this kind is to be so prepared that before they are laid on its masses are made capable of ejecting the axe and leaving no mark. As the material thus spread on proceeds to dry, lay on another, finer coat, so that a thick foundation of marble and white stucco, strengthened by polishing, may make a brilliant surface, evidence of your labour. For any walls that are diligently finished are unaffected by old age, and never lose the beauty of their colour when cleaned. For when walls that are still damp are adorned with paintings, they will dry out and the colour that is rooted in the fabric cannot be washed away.

22. On the polishing of concrete walls.

For cornice work a finer coating is necessary. It will need to be polished rather more, to give pleasure with a softer brightness. But you must take care that no gypsum is added to this coat. For it is a thirsty substance; and, while it is quickly drying out, seeing that the plasterwork of the cornice is applied to the polished surfaces of the walls and vaults, it will ruin the wall-faces around.

23. On the modelling of of cornices.

Walls in damp places are to be strengthened in the following manner. If continuous damp seeps through them, for 3 feet from its foot you are to clothe your wall with baked earthenware and then pound and polish this lining, so that it will be impervious to damp. But if there is a larger

24. On building concrete walls in damp places so that they will stay firm.

---

[1] Taking 'marmor grandi' to mean 'large-grained marble'.

qua collectus umor sine vitio parietis exeat. si autem affluens umor abundabit, tegulas bipedales ex ea parte qua umor inriguus erumpet diligenter picabis, ne vis umoris ad parietem transeat. ex altera parte, qua structurae iungentur, tegula calce liquida linietur, ut facilius operi adhaerere possit.

25. Triclinia hiberna minoribus picturis esse ornanda.
Vitr. VII, 4.

Triclinia hiberna non convenit grandibus picturis ornari, quoniam hibernis temporibus frequenti lumine cereorum aut lucernarum fumante obsolescunt. propterea et camerae eorum planae fiunt, ut detersa fuligine statim inluminatus splendor appareat.

26. Pavimenta ut in hieme tepeant.
Vitr. VII, 4
(Pall. I, 9).

Etiam pavimentorum utilis dispositio inventa videtur. itaque excavatis in altum duobus pedibus, festucato solo inducatur aut rudus aut testaceum pavimentum, deinde congestis et calcatis spisse carbonibus inducatur ex sabulone et favilla et calce mixta inpensa crassitudine unciarum VI. ad regulam exaequata planities reddit speciem nigri pavimenti. hieme ergo non recipit frigus et ministros licet nudis pedibus vapore delectabit. sic enim erit pavimentum ut etiam bibentium pocula si fusa fuerint momento siccescant.

27. De generibus colorum.
Vitr. VII, 6–14.

Colores vero alii certis locis procreantur, alii ex commixtionibus componuntur. rubricae itaque multis locis generantur, sed optimae in Ponto et in Hispania nascuntur. paraetonium ex ipso loco unde foditur habet nomen. eadem ratione et melinum, quod eius metallum per insulas cylcadas Melo dicitur. creta viridis pluribus locis nascitur, sed optima

DE DIVERSIS FABRICIS ARCHITECTONICAE

quantity of continuous damp, you will build a short channel,
rather below the level of the floor inside, where the water
can collect and run away without endangering the wall. But
if a great quantity of water wells up, you must carefully
spread pitch over the two-foot tiles at the place where the
water breaks out of the wall, so that no moisture may force
its way into the structure of the wall.[1] On their other face,
where they are attached to the wall, the tiles must be spread
with liquid cement, to give them a stronger adhesion to its
structure.

Winter dining-rooms are not suitable for decoration with
large pictures, for they are quickly dulled by the smoky
light from candles or lamps, which have to be numerous in
winter. So, too, their vaults have flat surfaces, so that one
can wipe the smoke off them and restore them to their
brightness.

Again, a practical way of laying out their pavements
seems to have been found. Excavate the earth to a depth of
2 foot, ram it down and put in rubble or a pavement of
earthenware. Then gather cinders and trample them into a
thick mass, and apply a layer containing a mixture of dark
sand, ashes and lime, and 6 inches in thickness. The surface
of this, brought to the level with a square, gives the appearance of a black pavement. So in winter time it does not
absorb cold; and its warmth will please your serving-men
even when barefoot. It will, too, be the sort of pavement
that will absorb in a moment the liquids spilt at drinking-
parties.

Now colouring materials are of two sorts, those found
naturally in certain places, and those that arise from artificial
mixtures. So red-ochres appear naturally in many places, but
the best in Pontus and Spain. *Paraetonium* (white chalk)
takes its name from the place where it is dug. In the same
way, too, Melian white is called so, because throughout the
Cyclades its mine is known to be on Melos. Green chalk is
found in several places, but the best chalk originated from

25. Winter
dining-rooms to
have no large
paintings on their
walls.

26. How to make
warm pavements
for the winter.

27. On the
different kinds of
colours.

[1] What I suppose to be the meaning of all this, I have stated at length in my
commentary.

75

creta Smyrnae tantum procreatur, quae graece Θεοδοτιον dicitur a Theodoto quodam in cuius solo primum est inventa. auripigmentum, quod αρσενικον graece appellatur, in Ponto nascitur. sandaraca plurimis locis generatur, sed optima in Ponto et iuxta flumen Hypanim. minii autem natura primum a Graecis Ephesiorum solo reperta memoratur, deinceps in Hispania. cuius natura has admirationes habet. glebae itaque cum ex metallis primum exciduntur, argenti vivi guttas exprimunt, quas artifices ad plures usus colligunt. neque enim argentum neque aes sine his inaurari potest. nam confusae in unum ita ut quattuor sextariorum mensuram habeant, centum librarum pondus efficient. supra cuius liquorem centenarium saxi pondus si posueris, sustinebit, scripulum auri super si posueris, in liquore descendet. unde intelleges non ponderis sed naturae esse discretionem. itaque si aurifex pannis textilibus adustum rudi vaso fictili solidi auri pulverem prius lavaverit, postea mixtum argento vivo vel in panno vel in linteolo comprimes ut liquor argenti expressus emanet et aurum solidum intrinsecus remaneat. verum probatio minii sic erit observanda. in lamna ferrea mittatur et super ignem ponatur tamdiu donec lamna rubescat. tunc retractum refrigescat. si colorem non mutaverit, optimum erit, si mutaverit, vitiatum erit. colores autem omnes calcis mixtione corrumpi manifestum est. chrysocolla a Macedonia venit, foditur autem ex metallis aerariis. armenium et indicum ab ipsis ostenditur quibus in locis nascitur. atramenti vero compositio sic erit observanda, quae non solum ad usum picturae necessaria videtur sed etiam ad cotidianas scripturas. lacusculus curva camera struatur. huic fornacula sic componitur ut nares in lacusculo habeat qua

Smyrna only. In Greek it is called *Theodotion* after a certain Theodotus, on whose property it was first discovered. Orpiment, which in Greek is called *arsenikon*, originates from Pontus. Sandarach is found in many places, but the best in Pontus and beside the river Bug.

But natural minium (red lead) is recorded by the Greeks as appearing first in the territory of Ephesus, and after that in Spain. It has the following remarkable natural characteristics. When clods of it are first cut out of the mines, they exude drops of quicksilver, which the workmen collect and put to various uses. For neither silver nor bronze can be gilt without their aid. For if you collect them into one mass of 4 pints, they will have a weight of 100 *lb*. But if you place above this liquid mass a hundred-pound weight of stone, it will hold it up. But if you lay on it a mere scruple of gold, this will sink into it. From which you can see that it is not the weight but the quality of the substance that matters. So if a goldsmith has washed off in a rude clay vessel the dust of solid gold that had been ironed on to woven clothes, you should next mix it with quicksilver and press the mixture inside a napkin or a linen cloth. Then the liquid quicksilver will be forced out, and solid gold will remain inside the cloth.

But this is how you should attend to the testing of red lead. Put it on an iron plate and place this over the fire until the iron has time to grow red hot. Then remove it and let it cool. If it has not changed colour, the red lead will be of high quality; but if it has, it will be impure. It is clear that all colours are impaired by an admixture of lime.

Chrysocolla (green malachite) comes from Macedonia, and is dug out of copper-mines. Armenian blue and indigo indicate by their names the places in which they are found.

This is how you must arrange for the manufacture of black pigment, which is not only clearly necessary as an ingredient in painting but also for our ordinary written documents. Build a receptacle with a domed roof. A small furnace is erected next to it so as to have vents into the receptacle, by which the smoke can penetrate. Burn pine

fumus possit intrare. taedae in eadem fornace incendantur, super taedas ardentes resina mittatur, ut omnem fumum et foliginem per nares in lacusculum exprimat. postea fuliginem diligenter conteres et aquam ad modum mittes et atramentum facies nitidum. pictores autem glutinum miscent, ut nitidius esse videatur. sed ad celeritatem operis etiam taedarum carbones cum glutino attriti parietibus praestabunt atramenti suavitatem, nec minus sarmenta exusta et contrita atramenti colorem imitabuntur. sedimenta uvae nigrioris si in optimo vino mersa arserint et postea exusta fuerint, addito glutino imitata indici suavitatem monstrabunt. usta vero, quae plurimum necessaria in operibus picturae videtur, sic temperatur. glebae silis boni in igne coquuntur, tunc acerrimo aceto perfuso extinguuntur, et reddunt purpureum colorem. caerulei temperationes Alexandriae primo sunt inventae, nunc autem Puteolis ex harenae pulvere et nitri flore temperatur aes cyprium adustum. cerussa et quam nostri aerucam vocant sic erit conficienda. sarmenta vitis amineae infuso aceto in dolio coniciantur, super tabulae plumbeae deponantur et dolium cludatur, et pluribus mensibus transactis aperiatur. sed cerussa in fornace coquatur, quae mutato colore meliorem efficiet sandaracam. ostrum autem quod pro colore purpurae temperatur plurimis locis nascitur, sed optimum insula Cypro et ceteris quae proxime sub solis cursu habentur. conchulae itaque cum circumcisae ferro fuerint lacrimas purpurei coloris emittunt, quibus collectis purpureus color temperatur. ideo autem ostrum est appellatum quod ex testis umor elicitur. qui cito ex salsugine inarescit, nisi temperatus umor melle circumfusus habeatur. fiunt etiam purpurei colores infecta creta rubiae radice. similiter ex floribus alii colores inficiuntur.

logs in this furnace, and throw resin upon the burning logs, that it may discharge all its smoke and soot through the vents into the receptacle. Later you will carefully scrape all the soot together and add water in due proportion, and so make a glossy black pigment. But painters add glue to it to add more apparent gloss. For quick work, however, the ashes of the pine logs, pounded together with glue will give walls a pretty blackness, just as burnt faggots pounded together will give a fair imitation of black pigment. Settlings of black grapes, which have been boiled dry in the best wine, and afterwards reduced to powdered ashes, will, if you add glue, imitate – indeed, display – the attractiveness of indigo.

But burnt cinnabar, which is very necessary in works of painting, is prepared in this fashion. Lumps of good-quality yellow ochre are roasted in the fire, which is then extinguished with very sour vinegar. They then yield a purple dye. The preparation of blue was first discovered at Alexandria, but now it is manufactured at Puteoli by the addition to scorched Cypriot copper of the dust of fine sand and the flower of natron.

White-lead and the substance that our craftsmen call verdigris are to be prepared as follows. Wood-chippings are to be thrown into a large jar, and vinegar of the wine of Picenum poured into it, strips of lead are to be placed on top, and the jar is then to be sealed up. After several months it is to be opened. But heat your white-lead in a furnace, and it will change its colour and give an improved variety of sandarach.

But the purple 'sherd-fish', which is treated to give purple dye, is found in a great many places. But it is at its best in the island of Cyprus and others nearest to the tropical zone. Now when you slit around the shells, they give out tears of a purple colour, which when collected result in a purple pigment. That is why it is called the 'sherd-fish', because the dye is drawn from its 'sherds'. It soon dries up because of its saltness, unless you hold in the moisture with a coating of honey. Purple colours are also created if chalk is tinged from the madder-root; and

itaque pictores cum voluerint sil atticum imitari, violam
aridam in vaso cum aqua ad ignem adponunt ut ferveat, et
decoctam in linteolo exprimunt et in mortario cum creta
conterunt et faciunt silis attici colorem. eadem ratione
vaccinium cum lacte temperantes purpuram faciunt elegan-
tem. qui non possunt chrysocolla propter caritatem uti,
herba quae lutear appellatur sucum caeruleum inficiunt et
utuntur viridissimo colore. haec autem infectiva appellantur.
propter inopiam coloris simili modo cretam selinusiam sive
anulariam vitro miscentes, quod Graeci ἴσατιν vocant,
imitationibus inficiunt indici colorem.

28. De normae
inventione.
(Vitr. ix praef.)

Quoniam ad omnes usus normae ratio subtiliter inventa
videtur, sine quo nihil utiliter fieri potest, hoc modo erit
disponenda. sumantur itaque tres regulae, ita ut duae sint
pedibus binis et tertia habeat pedes duo uncias x. eae regulae
aequali crassitudine compositae extremis acuminibus iungan-
tur schema facientes trigoni. sic fiet perite norma composita.

29. De horologii
institutione.
ex al. f. (cf. Vitr.
ix, 8).

Multa variaque genera sunt horologiorum, sed pelecini et
hemicyclii magis aperta et sequenda ratio videtur. pelecinum
enim horologium dicitur quod ex duabus tabulis marmoreis
vel lapideis superiore parte latioribus inferiore angustioribus
componitur, sed haec tabulae aequali mensura fiunt et quinis
lineis directis notantur, ut angulum faciant qui sextam horam
signabit. semis ergo ante primam et semis post undecimam
supplebunt xii numeros horarum. sed iunctis aequaliter ante
et extensis tabulis, in angulo summo iuncturae circinum
figes et angulo proximum circulum facies, a quo primum
lineae horarum partitae aequaliter notantur. item alium
maiorem circulum ab eodem puncto angulari facies, qui
prope oram tabularum attingat, ad quem aestivis temporibus

similarly other colours are made from flowers. So whenever painters wish to imitate Attic yellow ochre, they add a mass of dried violets to water inside a vessel, heat it up over a fire, and when it has boiled down strain it in a linen napkin. They then pound it with chalk in a mortar, and thus obtain the colour of Attic yellow ochre. In the same way by diluting whortleberry juice with milk they obtain an elegant purple. People who find malachite too expensive to use mix the plant called dyer's weed into blue dye and so obtain a vivid green. These colours are called dye-colours. Similarly, people who lack that colour will mix chalk of Selinus or 'ring chalk'[1] with the blue dye called in Greek *isatis* to obtain an imitation of indigo.

Since the principle of the square was a clever discovery and useful for all purposes – since, indeed, nothing can be done very practically without it, this is how you will prepare one. Take three scales, two of them each 2 foot long, the third 2 foot 10 inches. They are all to be of one uniform width, and are to be joined at the ends to give the shape of a triangle. Your square will thus be made to professional standards.

28. On the invention of the square.

The varieties of timekeepers are many and diverse.[2] But the principle of the double-axe and the semi-circular time-keeper seems clearest and best to follow. The double-axe timekeeper is called so because it is composed of two pieces of marble or stone, each broader above and narrower below. These blocks are made of equal size and are scored with five straight lines each. This will allow them to make an angle which will mark the sixth hour. Half a space before the first line and half a space after the eleventh will make up the number of twelve hours. Once one has joined the blocks evenly and laid them out, at the top angle of the join you shall fix your compass and make a small circle near the angle, from which the lines of the hours, evenly marked, are to start. Again, from the same point on the angle you are to draw another, bigger circle, which nearly touches the outer

29. On the making of a time-keeper.

[1] Not explained. Granger (*ad loc. Vitruv.*) thinks it is chalk from crushed beads.
[2] I am translating this chapter merely for the sake of completeness. I claim no merit for my efforts here.

gnomonis umbra pervenit. subtilitas ergo disparis mensurae
de spatio horarum expectanda non est, quando aliud maius
et aliud minus horologium poni solitum videatur, et non
amplius paene ab omnibus nisi quota sit solum inquiri
festinetur. gnomon itaque in angulo summo iuncturae
paululum inclinis ponitur, qui umbra sua horas designet.
constitues autem horologii partem qua decimam horam
notabit contra orientem aequinoctialem, sicut de exemplis
multifariam cognoscitur. horologium autem quod hemi-
cyclion appellatur simili modo de lapide vel de marmore
uno, quattuor partibus sursum latioribus infra angustioribus
componatur, ita ut ab ante et a tergo latiores partes habeat,
sed frons aliquantum promineat atque umbram faciat maiorem. sub hac fronte rotunditas ad circinum notatur, quae
cavata introrsus hemicyclium faciat schema. in hac cavatura
tres circuli fiunt, unus prope summitatem horologii, alius
per mediam cavaturam, tertius prope oram signetur. a
minore ergo circulo usque ad maiorem circulum horalem
una et x lineae directae aequali partitione ducantur, quae
horas demonstrent. per medium vero hemicyclium supra
minorem circulum planitia aequalis subtiliori crassitudine
fiat, ut aperta rotunditate digitali facilius solis radius infusus
per numeros linearum horas demonstret. hiemis ergo tempore per minorem circulum horarum numeros servabit,
aequinoctiali tempore medium circulum sequetur, aestivo
tempore per maioris circuli spatia gradietur. sed ne error in
construendo horologio cuiquam videatur, libero loco alto
vel plano sic ponatur ut angulus huius qui occiduas horas
notabit contra aequinoctialem vernum spectet, unde sol nono
kal. apriles oriatur. fit etiam in uno horologio duplex
elegantiae subtilitas. nam dextra ac sinistra extrinsecus in

edge of the blocks. The shadow of the gnomon reaches this circle in summer. Now you are not to expect any subtly uneven measure in the spaces given to the hours, since scales of different size normally seem to be arranged (according to season?), and nearly always men are in a hurry and merely inquire what hour of the day they are in. The gnomon that is at the top of the angle of the central join is laid with a slight inward (i.e. downward?) slope, to mark the hours with its shadow. You shall set up the sundial, so that the part with which it marks the tenth hour faces due east – a practice we see from many examples.

But the timekeeper which is called semi-circular must be made in a similar fashion out of one block of stone or marble, with four faces broader above and narrower below, so that its front and rear faces are larger. But let the upper edge nod forward a little, to make a larger shadow. In the shadow of this edge mark out a circle with the compass. When it is hollowed out, this will give the shape of a concave hemisphere. In this hollow three circles are drawn, one near the top of the dial, another round the cavity half way up, another round the cavity near its edge. From the small circle to the edge of the larger (on which the hours are written) draw eleven straight lines at equal intervals, to mark the hours. But across the cavity half way up, just above the smaller circle set a flat lid just equal to it in extent and of a delicate thinness. This is so that you can make a round hole in it one finger's width, and the sun's ray when it penetrates this can more easily mark the hours on the numbered lines. Now in winter time it will record the number of the hours on the smaller circle, at the equinox it will follow the line of the middle circle, but in summer time its march will cover the extent of the greater circle.

To prevent anyone thinking you have constructed a defective timepiece, erect it in an open space, whether on an elevation or on the level, in such a way that the corner which marks the hours of sunset stands and faces the sunrise of the spring equinox on 25 March. Moreover, one of these timepieces possesses a twofold elegance. For on its outer faces to

lateribus eius quinae lineae directae notantur, et ternae partes circulorum aequali intervallo sic fiunt ut una proxima sit angulis posterioribus, ubi stili ponentur qui umbra sua horas designent, altera mediam planitiem detineat, tertia prope oram contingat. has enim partes circulorum hieme vere et aestate sic ut interius gnomonis umbra sequitur. in angulis ergo posterioribus stilos modice obliquos figes, qui umbra sua horas designent. oriens enim sol in primo latere sex horas notabit, occidens alias sex in sinistro latere percurret. legitur etiam horas sic comparari debere, primam sextam septimam et duodecimam uno spatio mensuraque disponendas, secundam quintam octavam et undecimam pari aequalitate ordinandas, tertiam quartam nonam et decimam simili ratione edendas. est et alia de modo et mensuris horarum comparatio, quam prolixitatis causa praetereundam aestimavi, quoniam haec diligentia ad paucos prudentes pertinet. nam omnes fere, sicut supra memoratum est, quota sit solum requirunt.

Quantum ergo ad privatum usum spectat, necessaria huic libello ordinavimus. civitatum sane et ceterarum rerum institutiones praestanti sapientiae memorandas reliquimus.

left and right five straight lines are traced, and three arcs on each are drawn at equal intervals in such a way that one is very near the rear corners, where the rods are placed to give the shadow marking the hours, another occupies very nearly the line through the centre of the field, while the third falls near the edge. These arcs of circles the shadow of the gnomon follows in winter, spring and summer, just as it does the inside of the cavity. So on the rear corners you are to set up rods, that are slightly slanting, to mark the hours with their shadows. For the ascending sun will give you six hours on the first (or right hand) face, the descending sun six on the left hand face. I also read that the hours should be arranged and compared as follows: the first and sixth to be the same distance apart as the seventh and twelfth; again, the second and fifth as the eighth and eleventh; and finally, the third and fourth as the ninth and tenth. There is also another way of reckoning the limits and measures of the hours. But, since it would take time to tell, I have decided to omit it. For few sensible men take pains to this extent; since, as I said above, almost everyone asks to know only what hour he is in.

And so I have gathered in order for this little book of mine all the prescriptions useful for private practice. But I have left public institutions and everything of that sort to be related by a writer of outstanding wisdom.

A BRIEF COMMENTARY ON
M. CETIUS FAVENTINUS

I am not concerned to establish a perfect text of Faventinus, but only to discover the probable meaning and also the importance of the information that he has to give. I shall, of course, attend especially to its connection with similar material in Vitruvius and Palladius. I shall proceed in the normal way, by taking *lemmata* from the text; and for my purposes I still find the most convenient text in Rose's large edition of Vitruvius, of 1867. It is true that this relies on three manuscripts only, r, p and q (for which see p. xii of Rose's preface), and had not the benefit of the two codices soon afterwards discovered at Schlettstadt and Vienna (above, p. 2). But he seems to me to have used his material more sensibly than Krohn, whose Teubner (of 1912) was able to draw on both. However, I shall do my best to cite Krohn and others where there is any dispute of real substance.[1] After a century-and-a-half spent mainly in establishing their texts, Vitruvius and Faventinus could now, perhaps, benefit from a rather broader inquiry into their meaning and content.

TITLE

De Diversis Fabricis Architectonicae. See above, p. 1, n. 1. The real title, as given by MSS discovered in 1877, was apparently 'Artis Architectonicae Privatis Usibus Adbreviatus Liber'.

As for the numbers and headings of Faventinus' chapters, I do not think they are his own. See my remarks below, on chapters 18, 19 and 24.

---

[1] To do him justice, Krohn himself regards Rose's *editio maior* of 1867 as the fundamental text of Vitruvius. He observes, at the end of the preface to his Teubner edition, 'quod ea editio, sicut digna est, pro vulgata semper habebitur'.

CHAPTER I: ON THE DIFFERENT BRANCHES OF ARCHITECTURE

De artis architectonicae peritia multa oratione Vitruvius Polio aliique auctores scientissime scripsere. In any case, Vitruvius' *praenomen* has dropped out. Can we trust the readings here? It is important to notice that Faventinus knows of other authors besides Vitruvius. He actually claims in the next sentence to be retailing information from them as well – 'to dress up a few facts taken from them in an unvarnished prose for the benefit of private builders'. *privatis usibus*. Faventinus is surely alluding to Vitruvius' division of all architecture into 'public' and 'private' (1, 3, 1). He claims at the very end to have completed a treatise on private architecture – 'Quantum ergo ad privatum usum spectat, necessaria huic libello ordinavimus.' So his work is really a handbook for private builders.

quae partes itaque . . . cognosces. The proposed list of contents is adapted from Vitruvius with some intelligence, to make it suitable for the handbook. But their order is closer than Faventinus' own. Thus, in this initial paragraph the methods of finding water are mentioned last, just as in Vitruvius we do not encounter them until the eighth book. But in fact Faventinus soon reaches the topic, in his third chapter. Evidently he plunged into his preface before he had arranged his treatise.

quibusve mensuris aedificiorum membra disponantur. The proportions of the parts, so elaborately marshalled by Vitruvius, are in the upshot nearly all omitted by Faventinus. Those that he does give are strictly utilitarian or structural. The only exception is the shape of certain rooms (Chapter 14).

Peritus ordo discatur. I should prefer 'penitus'.

nam architecturae partes sunt octo. He has obtained the number by adding the three practical skills of building, siting and engineering (*aedificatio, conlocatio, machinatio*) to the five 'Greek' subdivisions of architecture given, with their Greek names, in Vitruvius 1, 2 (*taxis, diathesis, eurhythmia, symmetria* and *oikonomia*).

dispositio est apta rebus conclavium institutio. He apparently means a suitable arrangement of rooms. But this goes beyond

Vitruvius (I, 2, ii), who calls it a 'rerum apta conlocatio', and shows at once that he means their arrangement on the architect's drawing-board. Faventinus, genuinely puzzled, it seems, by this turn of meaning in Vitruvius, continues that *dispositio* (diathesis) is also the drawing up of the project for the future building – 'et operis futuri forma' – which needs to be shown three times, in plan (*ichnographia*), elevation (*orthographia*) and perspective (*scenographia*).

CHAPTER 2: ON WINDS

Eratosthenen . . . orbis terrae spatia esse metitum et sic certos ventorum didicisse flatus ('metitum' is post-classical). This goes even further than Vitruvius in deriving the directions of the winds from the circumference of the world. It also alleges that Eratosthenes connected the two. But Vitruvius (Rose 27) credits Eratosthenes with discovering the earth's circumference, not with any theory of winds. Here Faventinus has truly garbled his source.

tenere ergo orientem aequinoctialem, etc. S (the Selestadiensis, given by Krohn) confirms Marini's conjecture that a line had fallen out of the other codices in this sentence: 'tenere ergo orientem aequinoctialem ⟨subsolanum, meridiem austrum, occidentem aequinoctialem⟩ favonium, ⟨septentrionale⟩ sententrionem.' This, the text of S, is almost identical with Marini's conjecture. Clearly the word 'aequinoctialem' at the end of two consecutive lines confused the scribe.

'tenere ergo' depends grammatically on 'ferunt quidam philosophorum', and implies that some philosophers believed that four winds blew from the cardinal points of the compass. This corresponds to Vitruvius' 'nonnullis placuit esse ventos quattuor' (Rose, 24, 26). But the language and context of this passage also imply that Eratosthenes agreed with them.

inter ceteros tamen Andronicus Cyrrestes cum octo ventis orbem terrae regi adseverasset. All MSS, including S, read 'Androgeus Cyrenensis', and have to be corrected from the better MSS of Vitruvius. The account of Andronicus' views, which follows, comes very close to that in Vitruvius I, 6 (Rose 25).

sed plerique duodecim ventos esse adseverant. This is different from Vitruvius, who in his most detailed list of winds (Rose 27)

gives twenty-four in all, two 'blowing about' each of Andronicus' eight principal winds.

ut est in urbe Roma Triton aeneus cum totidem thoracibus ventorum factus. Evidently the source of Faventinus' information. This monument must have been erected after Vitruvius' time. It seems to have vanished without trace. But a monument from Rome survives, showing twelve winds, the dodecagonal base (*IG* XIV 1308) now in the Vatican, with the name of a wind on each face, reading clockwise from due north as follows: 'Septentrio, Aquilo, Vulturnus, Solanus, Eurus, Euroauster, Auster, Austroafricus, Africus, Favonius, Chorus and Circius' and, in Greek, 'Aparkias, Boreas, Kaikias, Apheliotes, Euros, Euronotos, Notos, Libonotos, Lips, Zephyros, Iapyx and Thrakias'. The upper face of the monument is apparently the flat *pelecinum* (cf. Chapter 29) figured on p. 259 of Soubiran's Commentary on Vitruvius' ninth book. According to Kaibel in 1G, it was found in 1779 in Rome, near the church of San Pietro in Vincoli. It confirms that at some date there was a fashion in classical Rome for twelve winds.

The 'thoraces ventorum' surely mean only the 'singuli lateres' of the polygon below the Triton. This is the simpler phrase used by Vitruvius for the sides of the Tower of the Winds (Rose 25).

ad exemplum Andronici Cyrrestae. 'exemplum', the correct reading of S, had not been anticipated by the editors. They had all been content with the 'templum' of the other codices, and had supposed Faventinus ignorant of the Tower of the Winds.

observabis ergo ne ianuas aut fenestras contra nocivos flatus facias. This is not so close to Vitruvius I, 6 (the source for most of this chapter) as to VI, 7 (Rose 144), which retails some examples of the damage done.

frigorosis ergo regionibus a meridie . . . ianuas et fenestras facies. This is taken from Vitruvius VI, 1 (Rose 134). Faventinus thus in this chapter shows his ability to select relevant material from all parts of Vitruvius and rearrange it intelligently. We can be grateful to him, too, for his additional information on the Winds and the Triton.

CHAPTER 3: ON FINDING WATER

*in sabulone masculo et harena et carbunculo certiores et salubriores
... sunt copiae aquarum.* For most of this chapter Faventinus
closely follows Vitruvius VIII, I (Rose 185ff.). Here there is a
variant. All texts of Faventinus read 'salubriores'. Texts of
Vitruvius either read, with G, 'certiores et stabiliores sunt copiae',
or omit 'et stabiliores' with H and S. The disagreement, then,
seems to go back to Faventinus.

Should we delete, with Krohn, the 'et' between 'harena' and
'carbunculo'? Neither he nor Rose cites the evidence of the
codices. But in Vitruvius G and H both read 'harenaque carbunculo', and 'et' is an addition of Fra Giocondo. According to
Krohn's text, then, Vitruvius thought of 'carbunculus' as a sort
of sand. Faventinus does so in his eighth chapter, where he
separates it from black and red pit sand. I have argued in my
Introduction (above, p. 34) that he thought of it as a pale sand – a
meaning anathema to the dictionaries.

*quoniam autem in lacunis similia nascuntur, facile his credendum
non est.* This is obscure. Faventinus is arguing that we cannot
trust the signs of a damp soil (alders, rushes, etc.) as proof of a
spring. For they grow equally in mere depressions of stagnant
water. Vitruvius is much more explicit (VIII, I, iii; Rose 186). He
says that such plants seed themselves during wet winters in
depressions which hold the damp a long time but have no proper
springs. He too uses the word 'lacunae' for these hollows.
Faventinus is copying Vitruvius, but for once his brevity becomes
too obscure.

CHAPTER 4: THE DIGGING AND LINING OF WELLS

Faventinus treats of this, logically, before he comes to the
piping of water supplies; whereas Vitruvius had treated of piping
and aqueducts first. In any case, on the normal country estate,
which Faventinus envisages, well-digging will be most important.
The detailed instructions for sinking the well and lining it with
opus signinum are derived in part from Vitruvius' instructions for
cisterns, in part (e.g., the diameter of the well and the thickness of
the lining) from the experience of Faventinus' contemporaries.

See pp. 18ff. of my essay. Faventinus even, after giving the right amounts for Vitruvian concrete, proceeds to specify the ingredients he would prefer himself. Krohn excises this passage (*sed licet auctores ad quinque partes harenae . . . testaceis operibus facies*). But there is no MS warrant for this; and it seems to spring chiefly from a determination to see nothing original in Faventinus.

redivivas expensas. 'Expensas', according to the Lexica, is very late Latin.

similiter et in testaceis operibus facies. Has 'omnibus' been omitted before 'testaceis'? This is the first brickwork structure that Faventinus mentioned. If it were inculcating a general rule, this sentence would have some point. As it stands, it is baffling.

aut harena rubrica. Better 'lubrica'? 'If the sand is slipping'.

CHAPTER 5: PROOFS THAT A PARTICULAR WATER-SUPPLY CAN BE USED

From Vitruvius VIII, 4 (Rose 204–5).

CHAPTER 6: THE CONVEYANCE OF WATER

aut tubis vel canalibus ligneis. A suitable method for country estates, but an addition to the three methods given by Vitruvius (Rose 206, 23). See Introduction, p. 29.

specus sub terra erit structura aut roboreis canalibus aquae ductus componatur. Post 'erit' supplevit Krohn 'fodiendus et'.

Manuscripts agree on the text, though p has been converted to 'uti specus sub terra erit struendum'. Faventinus is worried about the problem of getting the water around or through an intervening hill.

Vitruvius does not mention wooden channels. Faventinus, if he had pierced a tunnel through a hill, would hardly line it with a mere wooden pipe. I suspect that he recommends taking the water round the hill in wooden pipes or troughs, although Vitruvius, admittedly, recommends winding channels only for circumventing certain depressions (Rose 208, 15). So I dislike Krohn's reading 'aquae specus sub terra erit fodiendus et structura aut roboreis canalibus aquae ductus componatur'. Admittedly, Pliny tells us (*N.H.* XVI, 224) that water pipes of pine, pitch-pine and alder quickly perish unless packed closely into the

earth ('obrutae terra'). But he does not mention oaken pipes at all; and known underground pipes seem to be mostly of metal (e.g., the lead pipes under the *decumanus* of Ostia).

structura solida vel arcuatili ad libramentum aquae occurratur. The support for the water-channel is to keep it precisely on the exact line of slope from the spring to the final distribution-head. (For this meaning of 'libramentum', cf. Vitruvius – Rose 207, 1.)

aut fistulis plumbeis aut canalibus libere cursus dirigatur. The course will be free because it will not have to conform to the exact line of slope. So I reject Krohn's reading 'librate'.

aliquanto inferius planitia inflexa libretur, ut veniens aqua fracto impetu lenius decurrat. Clearly, a winding course is to break the rush of the water, where it starts from a spring high up on a slope. It should be a horizontal course with many twists and turns, contrived to break the impetus of its first rush downhill from the spring – a small version of the Euphrates at Babylon (Hdt. 1, 185). Compare the Roman aqueduct at Pergamum (Graeber, *Wasserleitungen von Pergamon*, Pl. 2). There seems to be nothing in Vitruvius resembling these instructions. As so often, Faventinus seems to be thinking of rather makeshift arrangements on a country estate. In his next sentence ('aut si longius de monte ducitur, saepius flexuosas planities facies') he is merely saying that on long descents you have to repeat these stretches of horizontal, winding pipe several times.

sed ipsi tubuli ex una parte angustiores fiant. Rough and rustic compared with their jointing in Vitruvius. See Introduction, p. 30.

CHAPTER 7: NAMES AND WEIGHTS CORRESPONDING TO SPECIFIC ADJUTAGES

The chapter follows pretty closely Vitruvius VIII, 7 (Rose 207–8). Many of the figures for the weights have been badly corrupted (see Rose and Krohn). Without Vitruvius' text, we could not restore them. Even in Vitruvius (Rose 208) they have suffered some corruption, but enough remains to show that the hundred-pipe, over a ten-foot stretch, weighed 1200 *lb.*, the corresponding stretch of ten-pipe 120 *lb.* The thickness of the lead wall must have stayed constant. Faventinus, followed by Palladius IX, 12, omits the ten-pipe and the five-pipe. But

Palladius evidently transcribed with intelligence the figures available to him. Like Faventinus, he mentions only one of the smaller pipes, the eight-pipe. But while not only Faventinus but the best texts of Vitruvius himself (G and H), not to mention Pliny (*N.H.* 31, 58) all give it a weight of 100 *lb.*, Palladius gives it the correct arithmetic weight of 96 *lb.*

CHAPTER 8: TESTING THE QUALITY OF SAND

For the difficulties in this chapter, see the appendix to my Introduction. For once, Krohn and Rose are agreed as to the text and the two additions to be made ('quae autem terrosa fuerit, non habebit asperitatem' and 'fossiciae ... propter pinguetudinem non conveniunt'). I have argued that on the whole this chapter makes perhaps some advance on Vitruvius in practical knowledge, and that it will give sense and possess an explicable relation to Vitruvius and Palladius if we believe that the 'carbunculus', one of the three sands that it describes, was not red, but some other ashen colour.

marina harena ... hoc vitium habet, tarde siccat. From Vitruvius. The statement is important, as showing that the Ancients aimed at quick-drying concrete. It is often believed today that pozzuolana dried slowly (nowhere do the Ancients say so – indeed, if it is their 'pit-sand', they say the opposite), and that they endured this for its other virtues. Our texts seem to contradict this.

CHAPTER 9: TESTING THE UTILITY OF LIME

For this, too, see the appendix to my Introduction. Faventinus shows a greater empirical knowledge than Vitruvius of the different kinds of lime.

CHAPTER 10: HOW TO MAKE SUN-DRIED BRICKS

Compare Vitruvius II, 3 (Rose 38) – on the whole, very close.
sabulone masculo. The adjective 'masculus' must surely refer to the relative roughness of the sand. Faventinus seems to think it had a desirable lightness ('levitas') rather than smoothness ('levitas'). For he remarks that chalk, red earth and *sabulo masculus* 'propter levitatem fortiora sunt operi. cetera genera quoniam aut gravia sunt aut paleas non continent ... fabricis inutilia videntur'. The point is of some interest, as modern

translators think that Vitruvius meant 'smoothness'. Granger, for instance, has the rather difficult translation, 'Bricks are to be made ... even of rough gravel. For these kinds, because of their smoothness, are durable.' Morgan tried to evade the verbal contradiction, not very successfully, by making the *sabulo* a 'coarse grained gravelly clay'. For Vitruvius himself, toughness and firmness were quite consistent with a light weight, as he makes clear just afterwards in describing pumice-stone (Rose, 39).

CHAPTER 11: ON PREPARING BRICK WALLS FOR THEIR FINAL COATS

Latericii parietes tribus inductionibus prius solidentur. Walls of mud-brick are to be strengthened by the applications of three coats, before a flawless coat of fine plaster ('opus tectorium') can be laid on. And they are to set hard, before this last coat is applied.

This advice is brief to the point of obscurity. Recent editors, who derive all this chapter from Vitruvius II, 8 (Rose 53), have not apparently noticed that it is even closer to VII, 3 (Rose, 167), which alone mentions the three preliminary coats – 'namque sic emendata tectoriorium in picturis erit species. subarescente, iterum et tertio inducatur, etc.'

We see the diligence with which Faventinus has read Vitruvius, and the care with which he gathers from widely separated passages the material relevant to any particular point in his own compendium. The rest of the chapter, on the lofty structures of *parietes caementicii* in Rome (where mere mud-brick walls would by no means fit the bill), and on the need to protect mud-brick walls with several crowning-courses of baked brick, is all taken directly from II, 8 (Rose, 52–3). Faventinus repeats the total height desirable for these courses, $1\frac{1}{2}$ foot, given by Vitruvius (Rose 53, 5).

CHAPTER 12: ON THE USES AND PREPARATION OF TIMBER

I have discussed this fully on pp. 5ff. of the Introduction.

a castello laricino est dicta. So all texts, and also Isidore *Or.* XVII, 7. This may be of interest, since 'larignum', the reading in Vitruvius II, 9, xv (Rose, 59), gives us a place otherwise unknown. (For the omission of Roman *insulae*, see below, on Chapter 14.)

CHAPTER 13: ON SITING THE DEPENDENCIES OF A
COUNTRY VILLA

Primo ita cortes et culinae calidis locis designentur. This is a
slight but apparently intentional alteration of Vitruvius' advice
(VI, 9: Rose, 146), 'in corte culina quam calidissimo loco designe-
tur'. Notice also the good example of the use of *cors* (*cohors*) in
its original meaning of a confined open space – our 'court'.

latitudo (sc. *bubilium*) *XV pedibus disponatur et* ⟨*in*⟩ *singulis
paribus VIII pedes relinquatur.* in *omisit Krohn.*

Faventinus omits the *longitudo*, which, according to Vitruvius
(VI, 9: Rose, 146), depended on giving each pair of oxen at least
7 foot. So Vitruvius pictures the length of a normal stall (for two
pairs) as something over 14 foot, with the animals standing at
right angles to its longer axis. Its width, according to Vitruvius,
should be from 10 to 15 foot, determined evidently by the length
of the animals. Faventinus is not inconsistent with this, but
slightly more generous. 'Let a width of 15 foot be arranged, and
let each pair be left a length of 8 foot' – which will determine the
length of the stall. Faventinus allows an extra foot for manoeuvre
around each pair of animals.

The text has various corruptions and marginalia here, but this
seems to be its gist. The advice of Columella seems rather
different. He advises (I, 6, iv) that the stalls should be neither too
hot nor too cold ('Pecudibus fient stabula, quae neque frigore
neque calore infestentur') – and heat would indeed be the greater
threat in much of Baetica, his native province. So he enjoins
different stalls for summer and winter. He also thinks 10 foot
ample for the width of the stalls, allowing the animals to stand
up or lie down, and also allowing the ox-herd to pass round them
(apparently he had stalls for single animals in mind).

equilia ... obscuriora fiant ut securi equi pabulentur. Faventinus
has added this observation to his Vitruvian material.

ovilia et caprilia pro magnitudine agri disponantur. This is
vaguer than Vitruvius (Rose, 147, 20), who appears to give the
precise space for each animal, but is, as often, a little difficult –
'uti singula pecora areae ne minus pedes quaternos et semipedem,
ne plus senos possint habere'. An area 6 foot square inside the

fold is surely a little excessive. But what else can Vitruvius mean? For 6 square foot would be too little. The obvious places in writers *De Re Rustica* have offered me no light here.

Most of this chapter is from Vitruvius. But he modifies Vitruvius' instructions (Rose, 148, 5), 'si quid delicatius in villis faciundum fuerit, et symmetriis quae in urbanis supra scriptae sunt ... struantur', and merely says 'si quid melius et nitidius facere volueris, exempla de urbanis fabricis sumes'. Thus, as in nearly every case, he refuses to discuss mathematical proportions.

CHAPTER 14: ON PLANNING A HOUSE IN TOWN

This chapter keeps pretty close to Vitruvius VI, 4 (Rose, 144).

nam quaecumque africum spectant, etc. One of the few places where Faventinus has abbreviated Vitruvius (himself harsh) to obscurity. Vitruvius says that bedrooms and libraries should face east, because one uses them in the morning; and that in eastward-facing libraries books will not rot. 'nam quaecumque ad meridiem et occidentem spectant, a tineis et umore libri vitiantur', etc. By omitting the statement that in eastward-facing libraries books will not rot, Faventinus makes his 'nam' meaningless. We may notice, too, that by apparently making 'africus' a synonym for 'meridies et occidens', he contradicts his own second chapter, where, following Vitruvius I, 6, iv (Rose, 25, 12), he gives 'africus' (the Libyan wind) a limited range between *auster* and *favonius*. Even in this chapter, however, his carelessness is far from gross.

It is interesting that he should add nothing about tenement-blocks in cities. In view of his independence elsewhere, we may perhaps conclude that he follows Vitruvius so closely not out of servility, but because in his time *insulae* have had their day. After all, where Vitruvius, talking of the larch in II, 8, xvi (Rose, 60) had said that its use in Rome would prevent fires, 'tabulae in subgrundiis circum insulas si essent ex ea conlocatae', Faventinus in the corresponding passage of his twelfth chapter remarks that it is useful 'in omni fabrica', because 'ex ea adfixae tabulae subgrundae ignis violentiam prohibent'. *Insulae* are quietly omitted.

CHAPTER 15: ON THE PROPORTIONS OF ROOMS

This very short chapter, almost the only place where Faventinus discusses proportions, and where his poverty on the subject contrasts most strongly with the amplitude of Vitruvius, is discussed on p. 32 of my Introduction. It is entirely consistent with a date for Faventinus around AD 300.

CHAPTER 16: ON BATH-BUILDINGS

For most of this chapter and its relation to Vitruvius v, 10, on which it seems to mark some practical advance, see pp. 15ff. of my Introduction.

supraque laterculis bessalibus et rotundis pilae instruantur. et rotundis *Polenus, Rose;* vel rotundis *Codd.; omnino delevit Krohn.* On p. 15 of my Introduction I support Rose. His is the only reading that explicitly gives their shape and their size. Krohn's attempts to deny any advance between Vitruvius and Faventinus seem to me, here and elsewhere, misguided.

melius enim ignis per angustiora latitudinis cellarum operabitur. Faventinus has just repeated Vitruvius' prescription, that the width of the bathroom (*cella*) should be two-thirds of its length. But Vitruvius gives no reason, at any rate at this point (v, 10, iv; Rose, 126). Faventinus has apparently seen for himself the draughts created by narrowing a space – 'the fire will work more keenly where the width of rooms is narrowed'.

hypocausteria pro loci magnitudine cum piscinis in septentrione vel aquilone constituantur, et ab eadem parte maxime lumen fenestris admittatur. The advice to place the hypocausts and the adjacent hot bathing-pools on the north side is not to be found in Vitruvius, and is one of Faventinus' additions. *Hypocausterium,* too, is an alteration of 'hypocausis', the noun in Vitruvius. It is the technical Greek word, found in papyri, for the actual furnace, and is surely the most natural form available.

There is a dispute here between Rose and Krohn. By detaching from *hypocausteria* the two first words of the sentence, 'aestivis balneis', Krohn makes this advice on placing the bathing-pools and most of the windows on the north side applicable to all baths. The preceding sentence in Krohn is made to read 'lumen fenestris

ab hibernis aut meridianis partibus tribuatur aestivis balneis' – viz. 'Bathing suites for use in summer should be given windows in their north or south sides.'

Commonsense would make against Krohn. For while all bath buildings, according to their seasonal use, should be given north or south windows, hot baths for use in summer should have their bathing-pools and windows on the north side. The light and heat might otherwise prove unbearable. Palladius, too, agrees with Rose's text. For in I, 40 he prescribes that 'piscinales cellae in aestivis balneis a septentrione lumen accipiant, in hiemalibus a meridie.' It is true that Pliny's Tuscan Villa, intended apparently for summer use (v, 6, *ad init.*), had a hot bathroom projecting southwards to catch the sun ('sol . . . praesto est, caldariae magis; prominet enim'). But degrees of shelter from the sun were provided, and in any case the summer on this upland site was exceptionally temperate: 'aestatis mira clementia; semper aer spiritu aliquo movetur.'

On the whole, Rose, is to be preferred to Krohn.

balneum culinae coniungatur. See Introduction, pp. 13–14.

CHAPTER 17: ON THE VAULTING OF BATHROOMS

For a discussion of this chapter, see Introduction, pp. 22ff. I do not understand what vault it is with which Faventinus is comparing his 'planae camerae' in the phrase 'eadem ratione et planas cameras facies'. In Chapter 25 the words evidently refer to vaults that have no reliefs or coffers.

numquam vitiabit contignationes. I am often in difficulty over the word *contignatio*. In most places in Faventinus (e.g. the beginning of Chapter 19) it means a horizontal framework, especially of floor-joists. I have argued, too, in the *Annual of the British School at Athens* 1970, pp. 179ff., that in Vitruvius it always means this. In VII, 3, i, for instance (Rose, 166, 8), *tecta* and *contignationes* are carefully distinguished. Vitruvius pictures some baths immediately below the outer roof, others at least one storey below it and presumably lit, like some rooms in the Forum Baths at Pompeii (Mau-Kelsey, Figs. 87 and 88), by openings high in the end walls. It may even be significant that Faventinus omits *tecta*. Possibly he imagines his baths as low in the building, and tacitly anticipates

Palladius' principle (see p. 15 above) of placing them below the winter apartments. All this one could maintain, if one pressed the meaning of 'horizontal framework' (*sc.* floor-joists) for *contignatio*. But this I have not the courage to do. Is the meaning always so definite?

sudationes etiam praestabuntur meliores. This, the last sentence of the chapter, seems to be Faventinus' own. Presumably sweating will be more efficiently managed because insulation will be greater. As every student of their buildings soon learns, the Romans were past masters of insulation.

CHAPTERS 18 AND 19: ON LAYING PAVEMENTS

Here the numbers and headings of Faventinus' chapters, which are found apparently in r and p (see Rose, 286), seem unable to contain the lubricity of Vitruvius' argument. Vitruvius devotes Book VII, chapter 1 to the laying of two sorts of mosaic pavement, the one sort resting on the ground, the other on a framework of timber joists. He hastily describes the lower levels of the former, then devotes a more precise account to those of the latter, and finally describes in fair detail the upper layers of both – viz. (1) the layer of rubble and lime, (2) the so-called 'nucleus' of powdered pottery and lime, (3) the pavement proper, of mosaic or patterned marble slabs. Faventinus' argument follows Vitruvius' pretty closely, and reads straightforwardly. So it seems to be one of the later scribes who arbitrarily and erroneously separated his single chapter into Chapters 18 and 19, giving the first only the few sentences on the substructure of solid pavements, and also the inappropriate heading, 'De expolitionibus pavimentorum'. This seems inaccurate (below, p. 100), and in any case refers only to a small part of Chapters 18 and 19. On this evidence, the numbers and heads of chapters in Faventinus' manuscripts are not his own.

Vitruvius VII, 1 is substantially the source not only of Faventinus 18 and 19 but also Pliny *N.H.* XXXVI, 181ff.

We might expect Faventinus on this topic to mark some advance beyond Vitruvius. Many mosaic floors had been made in the intervening centuries, even for external promenades – for instance, the black and white mosaics on the upper floors of the

Baths of Caracalla.[1] But Faventinus shows fewer differences than we might have supposed.

(18) *supra inpensa testacea crassior inducatur.* This layer of baked earthenware, above the 'rudus' and below the 'nucleus', is to be thicker than the 'rudus'. But for Vitruvius the 'rudus' is to be at least 9 inches thick' ('id non minus pistum absolutum crassitudine sit dodrantis' – Rose, 163, 6.17), and the 'nucleus' above it is to make the 'pavement' not less than 6 fingers thick. (The Latin is obscure, but in the next sentence the tesserae or cut stones are called the 'finishing of the pavement' – 'exacta pavimenta'; and so in ours 'insuper ex testa nucleus inducatur . . ., ne minor crassitudine pavimenti digitorum senum' should surely have the meaning I suggest, remembering that 6 digits would be an enormous thickness for mere tesserae, but reasonable for 'nucleus' and tesserae together). The greater thickness of the earthenware layer in Faventinus is just what we should expect of third-century work.

(18) *tertio nucleus id est inpensa mollior inducatur, et politionibus insistat ne rimas inutiles operi relinquat.* The 'nucleus' is here what we should call the *matrix* of the tesserae. It is to be given a smooth polished surface, so that the pavement proper – the *opus* – above it shall have no cracks in it. This is surely a different process from the 'expolitiones pavimentorum' of the chapter-heading (see above, p. 99).

(19) *in contignationibus diligenter respiciendum est ut aequalitas soli dirigatur.* Vitruvius mentions no 'aequalitas soli'. Faventinus probably means merely that the floor should have a level footing. He omits Vitruvius' advice not to allow joists to rest on intermediate party-walls, if one wishes the whole floor to remain level above.

statuminibus ruderi seu novo sive redivivo ad duas partes una calcis miscentur. A deliberate alteration and simplification of Vitruvius' advice, according to which 'old' rubble should be mixed with lime in the proportion of the five to two, 'new' rubble in that of three to one. Faventinus believed in less aggregate and more cement. Should 'inductis' be supplied after 'statuminibus', as in Vitruvius?

---

[1] See Erika Broedner, *Untersuchungen an den Caracallathermen* (Berlin 1951), pp. 19–21.

exacto pavimento ad regulam et libellam. The 'pavement' is here merely the rubble layer, beneath both the earthenware 'nucleus' and the top surface of tesserae.

The subsequent instructions for the upper layers omit Vitruvius' remark (Rose, 163, 22) that they be built up to the proper gradient ('fastigia suam extructionem habuerint'). What is this gradient? For pavements in the open air, Vitruvius gives the amount a little later (Rose, 164, 23), as 2 digits in 10 feet – about 1 in 80.

sub divo maxime vitanda sunt finita pavimenta. Faventinus faithfully echoes Vitruvius' reservations, and continues with his advice for making such pavements where they cannot be avoided. He retains the size and shape of tile – 2 foot square, with grooved edges – recommended by Vitruvius, for an additional layer between the rubble and the earthenware 'nucleus'.

tabulas quammagnascumque marmoreas. This rather unexpected Latin word cannot, perhaps, tell us very much. I do not know why Faventinus objected to 'quantascumque'.

CHAPTER 20: ON THE TESTING OF LIME FOR WHITEWASH

This is all from Vitruvius VII, 2 (Rose, 165).

CHAPTER 21: ON RUSH VAULTS

asseres abiegni ad lineam . . . dirigantur. 'Asseres abiegni' is the reading of Rose, for the 'abstinei' of r, p and g, adopted by Krohn. 'Abstinei', otherwise not found in a Latin text, presumably means 'free from grubs'. The Thesaurus ignores its existence. The corresponding passage of Palladius (I, 13) shows no awareness of 'abstinei'. (See Introduction, p. 24.) Nor, surely, would Faventinus have introduced the word casually, without further explanation of the circumstances. So, on balance, I decide for Rose.

Faventinus here, then, ignores Vitruvius' objection to the silver fir, specifies, unlike Vitruvius, the scantling of the *asseres*, and alters their spacing from 2 foot to 1½ foot. I have discussed these and Faventinus' other alterations on pp. 23–4 of my Introduction. On the whole, Faventinus marks a considerable advance on Vitruvius.

ne plus habeant grossitudinis quam digitos tres. The word 'grossitudo', like 'grossiori' a few lines below, is surely a sign of late date. According to the Thesaurus, it is found in Faventinus, and otherwise in authors of the fifth and sixth centuries.

posteo primo manu inducatur inpensa pumicea. What is this layer of pumice that is first to be laid on by hand? Vitruvius has no mention of it, and according to Miss Blake (*Ancient Building Construction*, I, p. 41) it is unknown to Augustan architects. It is, however, used on the intrados of the Pantheon's dome (Rivoira-Rushforth, *Roman Architecture*, p. 126).

et trulliʒetur ut canna subigatur, deinde harena et calce dirigatur. The layer of pumice is to be laid on, so that the reed matting may be hidden (driven beneath it). Again Krohn follows r, p and g in a reading – 'subligetur' – discarded by Marini and Rose (for 'subigatur'). In this case the codices surely make nonsense. For the reed-matting has to be tied and pegged *before* the coats of scoriae and concrete are applied.

deinde harena et calce dirigatur. 'Then let the pumice-layer be given a straight edge with the sand-and-lime cement.' Faventinus clearly took Vitruvius' words 'deinde harena dirigatur' (Rose, 166 *ad fin.*) to mean 'make it straight with sand-mortar', 'harena' meaning the same as 'harenatum', the word for sand-mortar at the beginning of VII, 4. Faventinus is worth notice here. Granger translates Vitruvius 'Then sand is to be applied' (as if harena were a nominative), and Morgan 'Then lay on the sand mortar, and afterwards polish it off (meaning?) with the powdered marble.'

et laquearis operis vel delicatae ut arcuatilis camerae exemplis uteris. This is apparently describing the effects to be gained by adding bundles of reed. It seems to have no obvious prototype in Vitruvius VII, 3. But a search into its meaning and its possible sources in later Roman architecture must await a full investigation of the Vitruvian chapter. As it stands, Faventinus' phrase is hard to comprehend. In my translation, I have guessed at the meaning. Some vaults, so decorated, are shown by E. Wadsworth in *MAAR* IV.

CHAPTER 22: ON THE POLISHING OF CONCRETE WALLS

This chapter is close to Vitruvius VII, 3.

umidi enim parietes cum picturis desudescent, et operi obligatus color elui non potest. Vitruvius VII, 3, vii (Rose 168) says virtually the same thing – that paintings applied to wet plaster will remain for ever. Thus the Ancients fully understood the principle of fresco-painting, though Miss Mabel M. Gabriel had some doubts about their knowledge (*Augustus' Garden-Room at Prima Porta* (New York University Press 1955), p. 24).

CHAPTER 23: ON THE MODELLING OF CORNICES

Vitruvius VII, 3, iii, the source of this chapter, makes it clear that these are the cornices between the walls and the vaulted ceilings of certain rooms. This would not have been obvious from Faventinus.

Faventinus has altered Virtuvius' order. Whereas Vitruvius treated cornices as the lower border of the vaults, immediately after his account of these, Faventinus treats them as the upper edge of the walls. Faventinus also omits Vitruvius' argument that a heavy cornice will collapse, and contents himself with saying that a thinner, subtler plaster has a better sheen.

CHAPTER 24: ON BUILDING CONCRETE WALLS IN
DAMP PLACES, SO THAT THEY WILL STAY FIRM

The text makes no mention of parietes *caementicii* – a word appearing only in the heading. Compare my remarks on the headings of Chapters 18 and 19.

Faventinus apparently bases his prescriptions for damp-proofing walls, so that water will not affect their decorative inner faces, on Vitruvius VII, 4 (Rose, 169–70). But he wanders far from his source.

The first prescription follows Vitruvius. *Si perpetuus umor manabit*, etc. Faventinus implies that the wall is a single solid structure. In that case, like Vitruvius, he recommends that *opus testaceum* be applied to the inner face for a height of 3 foot from the floor.

The second remedy, to be used with more persistent damp, is not so clearly Vitruvian. *Canaliculum brevem extrues aliquantum a pavimento altius.* 'Build a short channel rather below the level of the paved surface, to allow the damp to collect and leave the room without damage to the wall.' 'Altius' here means 'deeper' or 'lower', as we see if we compare Chapter 26 ('excavatis in altum duobus pedibus'). We could clinch the issue from Vitruvius, were not Vitruvius' whole prescription more elaborate and somewhat different. For he talks of a channel lower than the level of the room ('canalis ducatur inferior quam libramentum conclavis fuerit'),[1] but it is to run along the foot of the cavity in what is effectively a massive cavity-wall, with openings (*nares*) to let out the moisture not only at the level of the *canaliculus* but also at the top.

The third remedy also differs from the Vitruvian. According to Faventinus, if the damp in the channel overflows, one must protect the whole wall from it by lining it with two-foot tiles. The wet side of these tiles is to be coated with pitch, the side on which they are embedded in the wall with wet lime. For wet lime is an adhesive. ('si autem affluens umor abundabit, tegulas bipedales ex ea parte, qua umor inriguus erumpet, diligenter picabis, ne vis umoris ad parietem transeat. ex altera parte, qua structurae iungentur, tegula calce liquida linietur, ut facilius operi adhaerere possit'.)

All Faventinus' prescriptions are consistent with a single, solid wall. But Vitruvius' third remedy for damp is again more elaborate and implies a cavity wall of sorts. Along the channel and opposite the outer wall are to be set brick piers, one palm distant from it. These are to support a whole inner wall of 'hooked' or 'breasted' tiles (*tegulae hamatae* or *mammatae* – I prefer the latter, as Mau actually describes inner wall-faces of what may well be called 'breasted tiles' – Mau–Kelsey, *Pompeii*, p. 181 – and the manuscripts of Pliny 35, 159 tell us that such tiles were invented for use in bath buildings. This inner wall will extend up to the ceiling. On the side of the cavity, the tiles will be coated with pitch, on the side of the room with lime and water, which will

---

[1] Nearly 2 foot below the level of the floor, to judge from VII, 4, v (Rose, 171, 14–17). See below, p. 106.

facilitate a coat of mortar and crushed earthenware. If I am right, Vitruvian cavity-walls had given place, when Faventinus wrote, to single-shell walls. This would be reasonable, given the improvement in the concrete. By the time of Faventinus, builders had long used a concrete which insulated without the need for cavities, and which was not weakened by moisture. The normal wall of imperial date, for all its refinement of technique, is not a cavity-wall.

CHAPTER 25: WINTER DINING-ROOMS TO HAVE NO
LARGE PAINTINGS ON THEIR WALLS

The obvious argument, that the soot from candles and lamps will often need cleaning off the walls, is again taken from Vitruvius VII, 4 (Rose, 171).

grandibus picturis: a translation of Vitruvius' typical 'megalographia'.

propterea et camerae eorum planae fiunt, ut detersa fuligine statim inluminatus splendor appareat. The vaults of the *triclinia* are, it seems, to be smooth and not in relief, so that they can be quickly cleaned. 'Eorum' can refer only to the *triclinia*. Thus, the nature and the position of the *planae camerae* are much clearer in this chapter than they were in Chapter 17. Nor has Faventinus really modified Vitruvius, who says that the vaulted ceilings should be smooth and bright ('explicata camera pura et polita' in Rose's text) and the cornice below them fairly plain ('nec camerarum coronario opere subtilis ornatus').

CHAPTER 26: HOW TO MAKE WARM PAVEMENTS FOR
THE WINTER

All the instructions, how to make them warm, porous and dark (so that no spilt wine will spoil them), come from Vitruvius. Moreover, this chapter, like all these concluding chapters of Faventinus, follows and precedes its neighbours in the Vitruvian order, quite unchanged. The two dimensions given (a depth of 2 foot for the whole excavation and of 6 inches for the mixed layer above the ashes) are both from Vitruvius. Faventinus omits only the drainage slope, to be given to the under pavement of rubble or earthenware, which forms the lowest level of the whole floor,

and the channel into which it drains. (Incidentally, this shows that
Vitruvius thought of the channel at the foot of his cavity-wall as
very nearly 2 foot below the surface of the floor of the room – see
above, p. 104).

CHAPTER 27: ON THE DIFFERENT KINDS OF COLOURS

Faventinus gives on the whole a very competent *résumé* of Vitruvius VII, 7–14. He indicates more clearly than Vitruvius the
practical purpose of his account, which is to show *where* one *finds*
the *natural* colours and *how* one *makes* the *artificial*. 'Colores vero
alii certis locis procreantur, alii ex commixtionibus componuntur.
rubricae itaque', etc. This is Vitruvius' purpose too, but he has
entangled it in a rigmarole about plaster and marble.

Faventinus follows Vitruvius' order of pigments fairly closely.
For instance, the notice of *minium* follows at once upon sandarach, the last of the 'natural' colours, which Faventinus has
presented all in Vitruvius' order.

By contrast, the natural colours in Pliny 35, 30 owe little to
Vitruvius. Their order, indeed, is almost Vitruvian – 'Sinopis,
rubrica, paraetonium, Melinum, Eretria, auripigmentum'. But
Vitruvius knows no colour called 'Eretria'. Nor does he or
Faventinus (who talks only of a good *rubrica* from Pontus) make
Pliny's distinction between *rubrica* and *Sinopis*. Moreover, just
before this sentence Pliny has made an important distinction,
unknown to Vitruvius, between 'colores austeri' and 'colores
floridi'. Finally, Pliny here excludes sandarach from the natural
colours and includes it among the manufactured. For Vitruvius
and Faventinus it is both mined and manufactured (from *cerussa*).
But Pliny shows in Chapter 39 that the sandarach alleged by King
Juba to be mined in the Island of Topaz certainly never reaches
Rome. I wonder from what mines Vitruvius' came.

As he continues his exposition, Pliny works in material from
many authors, including a line from the Fourth Eclogue. By
contrast, the derivation of Faventinus from Vitruvius alone is
here very striking.

rubricae itaque multis locis generantur. Faventinus begins his
list with this, omitting Vitruvius' account of *sil*, or yellow ochre.
But from *rubrica* onwards he keeps very close to Vitruvius VII, 7.

(However, he omits the Lemnian *rubrica*, praised by Vitruvius, whereas Pliny adds to the Lemnian the *rubrica* from Cappadocian caves – a source perhaps opened up between Vitruvius' time and his own.)

minii autem natura, etc. For the discovery and properties both of *minium* and of its attendant quick-silver, used in gilding, etc., Faventinus abbreviates Vitruvius VII, 8 but keeps faithful to its exposition.

colores autem omnes calcis mixtione corrumpi manifestum est. This is the only statement that Faventinus retains from the whole of Vitruvius' ninth chapter. This is surprising, as this chapter deals with the preservation of the *minium*'s redness against sunlight, by the waxing process called *ganosis* (for which see, e.g., Miss Richter, *Sculpture and Sculptors of the Greeks* (New Haven 1970), pp. 129–30). Faventinus passes to the manufactured colours, beginning with *atramentum* (used both in black paint and in ink).

Lacusculus curva camera struatur. huic fornacula sic componitur, etc. In Columella IV, 8, ii *lacusculus* means a 'little lake', in XII, 50, iii a 'bin'. Faventinus pictures the lacusculus as an appendage to the furnace (*fornax*); and the pine-resin is placed above the logs in the furnace, so that its smoke is wafted into the *lacusculus* through various vents, or *nares*, and collects there as the purest charcoal. *Lacusculus* appears in all the manuscript and printed texts of Faventinus.

But in the corresponding place in Vitruvius VII, 10 (Rose, 180, 6) we find not *lacusculus* but *laconicum*. Did Faventinus follow a corrupt manuscript, or did he give his own variant deliberately? Just as in Faventinus the furnace, containing the logs and resin, is adjacent to the *lacusculus*, so in Vitruvius the furnace (*fornacula*) is adjacent to a very carefully finished *laconicum*, and connected with it by vents. The smoke from the furnace is diverted through the vents into the *laconicum*, and adheres to its walls and curved vault ('circa parietem et camerae curvaturam adhaerescit').

Thus the processes in both authors are identical. It seems most likely that Faventinus did not understand the word *laconicum*, and translated it into a Latin term which sounded, and for his purposes meant, nearly the same. Incidentally, Vitruvius' word *curvatura* would apply as easily to a conical as to an hemispherical

vault. But in v, 10 (Rose, 126, 20ff.) he definitely uses the words *curvatura hemispherii* of his *laconicum*. Whether or not it was first applied by Agrippa (cf. Dio LIII, 27), the word *laconicum*, as used of bath-buildings, may have had a fairly short history.

usta vero, quae plurimum necessaria in operibus picturae videtur. Faventinus strangely reverses the order in which Vitruvius discusses *usta* (ochre reduced to purple) and caerulean blue. Moreover, he declares *usta* necessary for painting, while Vitruvius (Rose, 181, 7) had merely called it pretty useful in stucco-work.

nunc autem . . . temperatur aes cyprium adustum. It is clear from the context and from Vitruvius (Rose, 180, 30) that it is the mixture of sand and flowers of natron that is being tempered (rendered smooth and even), and that the copper is then added. Krohn marks a *lacuna*. Or could one simply read 'et aes cyprium additur', or, better, 'aduritur' – the climax of Vitruvius' long process of manufacture?

cerussa et quam nostri aerucam vocant, etc. Omnia post 'cerussa' delevit Krohn. 'et' supplevit *Rose*, ex Vitruvio. Though Faventinus' text is in some disorder hereabouts, that of Vitruvius, whom he is palpably following, makes everything clear. The processes, says Vitruvius (Rose, 181) of making white lead (*cerussa*) and verdigris (*aeruca*) are basically identical; to obtain the first one placed lead lumps, to obtain the second copper plates over wood-chips in closed jars. Rose, whose emendations of Faventinus give Vitruvius' sense, is surely to be preferred to the wholesale excisions of Krohn.

sarmenta vitis amineae infuso aceto, etc. Vitiosa mineae *codd*; delevit *Krohn*, correxit *Rose*. According to Vitruvius, at Rhodes, the centre of the manufacture, they put *sarmenta* (wood-chippings), vinegar and lead lumps in the jar. If Rose is right, Faventinus describes an identical process in his own day, merely adding that the vinegar is of the wine of Picenum (*vitis aminea*), as if, for him, Italy had replaced Rhodes as the centre of production. Curiously enough, Rhodes had been replaced for the next product, sea-purple (*ostrum*), by Cyprus, at least in the eyes of Faventinus.

plurimis locis nascitur, sed optimum insula Cypro, et ceteris, quae proxime sub solis cursu habentur. The phrase is almost the same as

Vitruvius (Rose, 182, 9), with the significant substitution of Cyprus for Rhodes. For Vitruvius 'hoc Rhodo etiam insula creatur ceterisque eiusmodi regionibus quae proximae sunt solis cursui'.

The rest of the chapter contains no important modifications of Vitruvius.

CHAPTER 28: ON THE INVENTION OF THE SQUARE (*Norma*)

Faventinus' 'Square' is an isosceles right-angled triangle, with an hypotenuse of 2 foot 10 inches, a side of 2 foot. $2\frac{5}{6}$ is very nearly the square root of 8. These dimensions are not those of Vitruvius' *norma*, which are the time-honoured 3, 4 and 5 foot (Book IX, Preface; Rose, 214). Clearly, Faventinus' new dimensions are far more useful for his favourite *tegulae bipedales*, also with faces 2 foot square, which are so important, for instance, in Chapters 16 and 24.

CHAPTER 29: ON THE MAKING OF A TIME-KEEPER

I have neither the time nor the knowledge at present to comment upon this highly technical chapter, and the relation of its material to that in Vitruvius' ninth book. I would merely say that with characteristic modesty and good sense, Faventinus limits himself to two types of time-keeper, the *pelecinum* (or double-axe type) and the *hemicyclium* (apparently the common type with a half-hemisphere hollowed out of the two adjacent faces of a rectangular block). Jean Soubiran, the learned editor of Book IX, shows bias against Faventinus on p. 241, when he says (my italics) 'Il n'y a malheureusement rien à tirer de la notice que Cetius Faventinus, puisant *pour une fois* à une autre source que Vitruve, consacre à l'hemicyclium.' On the contrary, I hope this study has shown Faventinus' sturdy independence of Vitruvius. He has surely succeeded in his main undertaking, of which he reminds us in his last paragraph: 'Quantum ergo ad privatum usum spectat, necessaria huic libello ordinavimus.'

List of main additions and changes made by Faventinus to the substance of Vitruvius

Chapter 2   Twelve winds, in place of eight. The Triton at Rome.

Chapter 4   Transference of the lining of cisterns to the lining of wells. Faventinus gives the dimensions of the lined well, and would prefer a different proportion from the Vitruvian for the sand and lime in the mortar.

Chapter 6   Wooden pipes or channels for water, channels with a steep gradient and a winding course and tapered pipes.

Chapter 8   Specifies the kinds of limestone most suitable for concrete.

Chapter 12   The properties of the beech, cypress and pine.

Chapter 16   Changes in the structure of the hypocaust in baths, the layout of hot baths and the siting (next to the kitchen of the villa).

Chapter 17   The lower vault of Vitruvius' double suspended vault replaced by a tougher vault of concrete.

Chapter 19   Different proportions of aggregate and cement in concrete floors.

Chapter 21   Changes in the timbers used for rush-vaults, and in their spacing. Their scantlings given more precisely.

Chapter 23   Cornices included not in vaults, but in walls.

Chapter 24   Systems, different from the Vitruvian, of water-proofing walls. Faventinus apparently envisages solid walls, as opposed to Vitruvius' cavity-walls.

Chapter 28   Dimensions of the builder's square (*norma*) are altered from Vitruvius, to fit *tegulae bipedales*, etc.

INDEX

INDEX OF ENGLISH TECHNICAL TERMS

INDEX OF LATIN TECHNICAL TERMS

lignum Gallicum 6, 24
linea 70, 101
lutear 80

maltha 20
mammata *see* tegula mammata
marmor sectile 68
megalographia 105
melinum 74
miliarium 14
minium 77, 106, 107
modulus 40

nares 48, 78, 104, 107
norma 80, 109
nucleus 66–8

oecus 62
opus
    albarium 64, 70
    coronarium 72, 105
    figlinum 21
    laqueare 72, 102
    signinum 18, 20, 48, 90
    tectorium 54, 56, 64
    testaceum 19–20, 50, 72
orthographia 40
ostrum 78, 108
ovile 60, 95

palatio 58
paraetonium 74, 106
paries *passim*
patena 64
pavimentum 2, 66–70, 101, 104
    testaceum 9n, 20, 68, 74
pelecinum 89, 109
podium 9n
praefurnium 62
praetorium 16
pumicea *see* inpensa pumicea

quinarius 30n

receptaculum 52
regula 68, 74, 80
ridica 6
rubia 78
rubrica 74, 106
    Lemnia 107
rudus 66, 74, 100
    pedaneum 68

sabulo 74
    masculus 35, 56, 93
    solutus 44–5
sandaraca 76, 78
saxum
    album 54
    columbinum fluviatile 54
    rubrum 29n, 37, 44
scenographia 40
sil 78, 106
    atticum 80
silex 18, 37
solium 14, 64
statumen 66, 100
statumino 66
stilus 84
structura 18, 34, 37, 48, 50, 56, 74
    arcuatilis 30, 52
    caementicia 54
    solida 30
    testacea 19n, 25, 26
subgrunda *see* tabula subgrunda
subsolanus 42–3
sudatio 23, 66, 99
superfusio 20
suspensura 62

tabula 25, 68, 71n, 80
    subgrunda 58
tectorium *see* opus tectorium
tectum 98
tegula 62, 64, 68, 74
    mammata 104
tepidarium 14
tessera 68, 100
testaceum *see* opus testaceum, pavimentum testaceum
tignatio 68
torcular 8, 60
trullizatio 72
trullizo 64, 70, 72, 102
tubulus 52
tubus 50

uncia 74, 80

vaccinium 80
venter 26, 27 (fig.), 28–31
villa 24n
vir illustris 1
vitis aminea 78

INDEX OF GREEK WORDS

INDEX OF PROPER NAMES

Schmitt, J. C. 5n, 9n, 17n
Schmitt, V. G. E. 7n
Selestadiensis (codex 8) 1–2, 88, 89
Seleucia ad Calycadnum 21n
Semiramis 20
Septentrio 42–3, 60, 89
Sinopis 106
Sirch, M. 1n
Smyrna 76
Solanus 89
Soubiran, Jean 89, 109
Spain 11, 75, 77
Spalato 15
Suetonius 16
Syria 4, 5, 61

Theodotus 76
Theophilus 1
Thrakias 89
Topaz, island 106
Tower of the Winds *see* Athens
Triton 41–1, 89
Tunisia 61n

Tuscan Villa (Pliny's) 98

Van Deman, E. B. 34n
Varro, *De Agricultura* 6, 11
Veii 37
Vienna 1n, 2, 86
Vitruvius
    name 1, 40–1
    as water-man 30
    topics discussed in: baths 11–13 (fig.); cisterns 18; concrete 18; floors (of bath-buildings) 15; framed floors 98–9; pavements 101; pigments 106–8; proportions 32–3; timber-trees 3–4; vaults 21–2; waterproofing 103–5; water-supply 25–6, 27 (fig.), 28–9; winds 88; wine-cellars 8
Vulturnus 89

Wadsworth, E. 102
White, K. D. 11n, 38n

Zephyros 89

For EU product safety concerns, contact us at Calle de José Abascal, 56–1°,
28003 Madrid, Spain or eugpsr@cambridge.org.

www.ingramcontent.com/pod-product-compliance
Ingram Content Group UK Ltd.
Pitfield, Milton Keynes, MK11 3LW, UK
UKHW012338130625
459647UK00009B/369